Mastering Complex Rhythms for Musicians

Arjan .B Combs

All rights reserved.

Copyright © 2024 Arjan .B Combs

Mastering Complex Rhythms for Musicians : Unlocking the Art of Irresistible Beats: A Comprehensive Guide for Music Enthusiasts.

<u>Funny helpful tips:</u>

Cultivate inner peace; it's the anchor in life's storms.

Stay updated with literary festivals and events; they offer a pulse on current literary trends and discussions.

<u>Life advices:</u>

Stay connected with literary mentors; their guidance can shape your reading journey and insights.

Stay true to your word; integrity builds trust and respect.

Introduction

This is a comprehensive exploration of complex rhythmic concepts aimed at music producers seeking to elevate their compositions. This guide delves into the intricacies of tempo, duration, time signatures, meter, irregular meter, and introduces advanced concepts like polymeter and polyrhythm.

The Basics section lays the foundation by covering fundamental elements such as tempo, duration, time values, beaming, accents, and triplets. Understanding these basic components is essential for any music producer striving to create intricate and compelling rhythms.

The exploration of time signatures and meter provides a deeper insight into rhythmic structures, including duple, triple, quadruple meter, and their variations. The guide introduces both simple and compound meters, offering a comprehensive overview of rhythmic possibilities.

Irregular meter challenges conventional rhythmic norms, introducing quintuple and septuple meters, as well as other irregular metric patterns. This section encourages music producers to break free from traditional constraints and explore diverse rhythmic expressions.

Moving towards a variety of rhythms, the guide explores syncopation, tuplets, triplets, and more complex rhythmic elements. Additive meter is introduced, emphasizing its application in music production using DAW (Digital Audio Workstation) software and stress programming.

The guide then delves into the intricate realms of polymeter, providing historical context and practical examples. Music producers are guided on how to incorporate polymeter into their compositions, with detailed examples and insights on anchoring and truncating polymeters for effective integration.

Polyrhythm, another advanced rhythmic concept, is thoroughly explored. The guide covers elements of polyrhythms, including 3:2 and 4:3 polyrhythms, progressing to more complex variations. Practical applications of polyrhythms in DAW software are also discussed, providing producers with the tools to implement these sophisticated rhythmic patterns.

This book serves as a valuable resource for music producers looking to expand their rhythmic vocabulary. With a blend of theoretical knowledge and practical applications, this guide empowers producers to experiment with complex rhythmic structures, ultimately enhancing the depth and creativity of their musical compositions.

Contents

CHAPTER 1: THE BASICS 1
    Tempo 2
    Exercises 4
CHAPTER 2: DURATION 5
    Time values 5
    Beaming 11
    Accents 12
    Triplets 13
    Exercises 15
CHAPTER 3: TIME SIGNATURES 18
    Exercises 22
CHAPTER 4: METER 23
    Duple, Triple and Quadruple Meter 26
    Simple Meter 26
    Simple Duple Meter 27
    Simple Triple Meter 31
    Simple Quadruple Meter 33
    Compound Meter 34
    Compound Duple Meter 35
    Compound Triple Meter 40
    Compound quadruple meter 42
    Recap 44
    Exercises 45
CHAPTER 5: IRREGULAR METER 46

Breaking the Mould 46
Quintuple Meter 47
Septuple Meter 51
Other Irregular Metric Patterns 53
Exercises 54
CHAPTER 6: TOWARDS AVARIETY OF RHYTHMS 55
Syncopation 55
Tuplets and Triplets 58
More complex tuplets 61
Exercises 62
CHAPTER 7: ADDITIVE METER 63
Use of additive meter 71
Use of additive meters using DAW software 72
Stress programming 75
Exercises 77
CHAPTER 8: POLYMETER 79
The history behind the use of polymeter 79
Using polymeter in your music 80
Example One: 8:5 81
Example Two: 16:3 82
Example Three: 9:7:4:3 83
Session View 84
Anchoring 86
Truncate your polymeters 87
Exercises 89
CHAPTER 9. POLYRHYTHM 90
Elements of polyrhythms 91

3:2 polyrhythms 94
4:3 polyrhythms 96
More complex polyrhythms 97
Use of polyrhythms in DAW software 98
Examples of Polyrhythm in Action 102
Example One: Shuffled Percussion Track 103
Example Two: Triplet Hi-hats vs 4/4 Open Hi-hat.............................103
Example Three: Curtailed 7:4 104
Example Four: 5 vs 4 vs 3 105
Exercises 106

CHAPTER 1: THE BASICS

Polyrhythm and polymeter are two phenomena that should be part of your music production repertoire. This is because they open a fascinating world of rhythmic invention and possibility. In this book, I will show you how to harness these phenomena in your own productions.

To understand and use them, some preparation is needed—especially for those whose experience in using meter might be limited to only four beats to the bar.

Most music has a continuous pulse running through it. Many musicians refer to this pulse as the beat. This beat can be anything from the subtle pulse implied when someone plays an acoustic guitar to the strong pulse of the kickdrum in House and Techno. However, the beat is also at play when we feel the tension built by the fast, staccato notes of a snare drum roll, or when we *feel* that a piece of music is about to finish. The beat gives us that intuitive map of what we expect from a piece of music.

This beat proceeds not only cyclically, it also does so on many fractal levels. Each time cycle contains other lesser cycles within itself, while often being a part of a greater cycle—rather like a tree in which the trunk divides into branches, and these branches divide into smaller branches.

This fractal nature of musical time is the reason that notes are input and stored in DAW software using a grid, as shown in Figure 1.1:

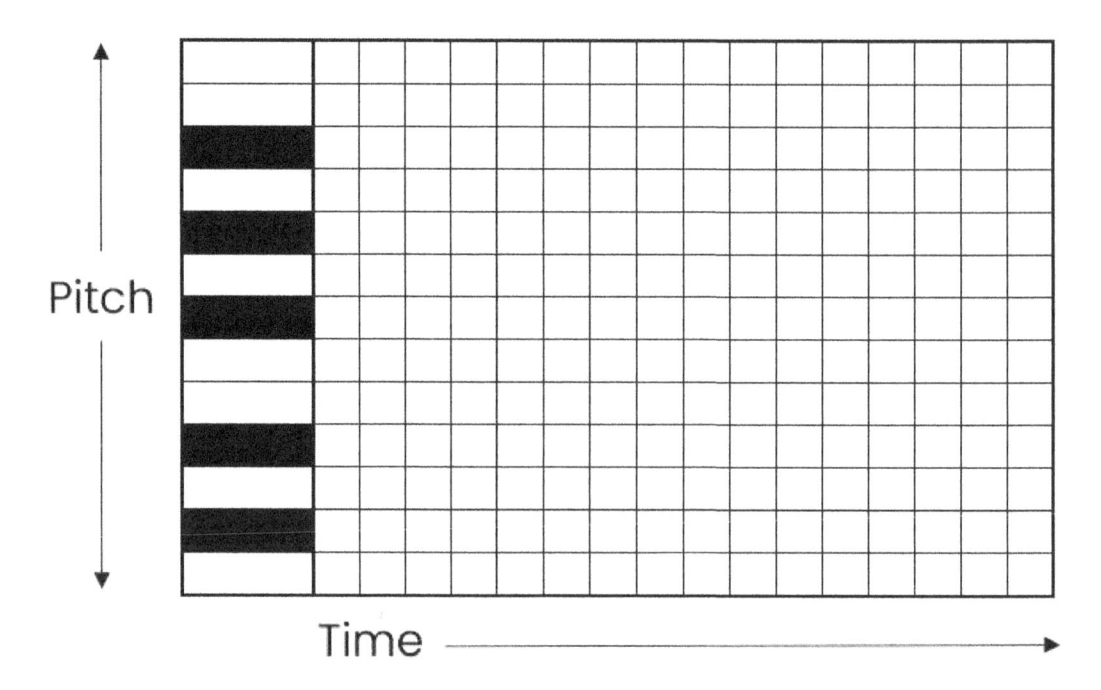

Figure 1.1: Within the grid in DAW software, time runs horizontally, with pitch running vertically, creating a two-dimensional view of notes.

Tempo

So far as discrete musical time is concerned, the beat acts as a driver, imparting to the music a sense of propulsion and forward movement through the journey of the music.

Although the beat may be a regular one, the length of each beat is key. In some pieces of music, the beats are sparse. This produces a perception in the listener that the music is moving at a slow speed. In other pieces, the beats are dense, which produces the feeling that the music is moving at a fast speed.

The name for this quality of the music is *tempo*, which is the speed at which the music should be played. During the classical era of music, tempo represented a stylised feature of musical expression, and it was denoted by Italian terms, such as *adagio* (slow), *moderato* (moderate) and *presto* (fast). There was always some margin of flexibility for the performer to interpret these tempo designations in their own way.

Tempo, as a more exact feature of our music, only really developed with the invention of the metronome. This was a mechanical device with a moving arm that ticked at the exact speed at which the music is to be played, as shown in Figure 1.2.

Figure 1.2: A metronome allowed for more precise measurements of musical tempo.

The speed itself could then be represented by how many of these beats occurred each minute, i.e., beats per minute. A tempo of 180 beats per minute was fast, a tempo of 100 beats per minute was moderate, and a tempo of 40 beats per minute was very slow.

We use the same measurement of tempo these days, with each genre having its own tempo expectation. This is shown in Table 1.1:

Table 1.1: A range of expected tempi for various contemporary music genres.

Genre	BPM range
Hip Hop	85-95
Nu-Disco	105-120
House	115-125
Techno	120-140
Dubstep	135-145
Drum and bass	160-180

Another fundamental building block of musical time is duration. We shall explore this in the next chapter.

Exercises

1. Write a drum track, then move the tempo of your DAW around while it is playing, all the way from its lowest possible setting to its highest. Reflect upon the experience—at what extremes of tempo does your drum track cease to make sense?

CHAPTER 2: DURATION

There are two important factors that govern the placement of sound events, such as notes, within a piece of music. The first is the location of the sound event as a part of the track. This location is calibrated in terms of bars, beats and sub-beats. The second is the duration of the sound event.

To get a handle on these parameters, it is vital for us to understand how musical time is partitioned, along with the signs and symbols that are used to represent those partitions. Fortunately, if you have a grounding in Western music theory and can read written music, you can skip to Chapter 3. If you don't, it is worth learning the time values given in this chapter. The music theory in this book is impossible to articulate without at least some grounding. Fortunately, it's very easy to learn, and will be useful to you throughout your musical career!

Time values

In Western music, duration is represented by a series of *time values* that signify units, multiples or divisions of a beat. As a music producer, you'll no doubt have used these time values in your own work.

First, there is the *whole note*. Drawn into the piano roll of the DAW, you notice that this whole note lasts for a full four beats, or a single bar of the track, as seen in Figure 2.1:

Figure 2.1: A whole note within a bar of 4/4.

The whole note's symbol is shown in Figure 2.2:

𝐨

Figure 2.2: The whole note's symbol.

Each whole note can be divided into two half notes. In written music, these are represented by the symbol in Figure 2.3:

𝅗𝅥

Figure 2.3: The half note's symbol.

They are written in your DAW software as shown in Figure 2.4:

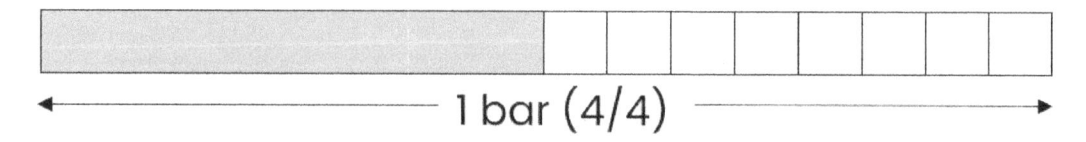

Figure 2.4: A half note within a bar of 4/4.

Each half note is divisible into two quarter notes. In written music, they appear as shown in Figure 2.5:

♩

Figure 2.5: A quarter note.

On the piano roll, a quarter note would thus appear as in Figure 2.6:

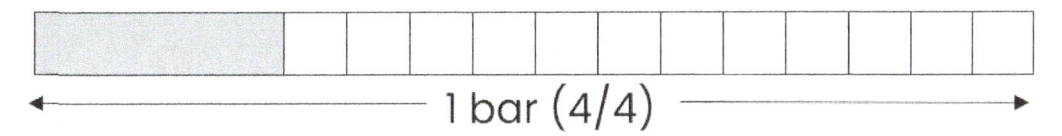

Figure 2.6: A quarter note within a bar of 4/4.

The quarter note is the pivot between longer note durations and shorter ones. This is because quarters represent the basic beat of contemporary music. To appreciate this, just think of the underlying pattern upon which many drum tracks are based. At a bare minimum, there is a kick on beats 1 and 3 and a snare on beats 2 and 4. Kick-snare-kick-snare—each of these hits occurring at the commencement of each quarter note beat of the bar.

Each quarter note is divisible into two eighth notes, which, in written music, are represented by the symbol in Figure 2.7:

Figure 2.7: An eighth note.

In a DAW, they appear as shown in Figure 2.8:

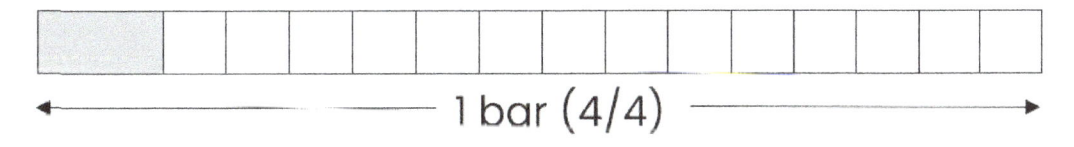

Figure 2.8: An eighth note within a bar of 4/4.

Each eighth note is similarly divisible into two sixteenth notes. In written music, they are represented by the symbol in Figure 2.9:

Figure 2.9: A sixteenth note.

These look like eighth notes, but they have two flags attached to the tail of the note, rather than one. These appear on the piano roll as shown in Figure 2.10:

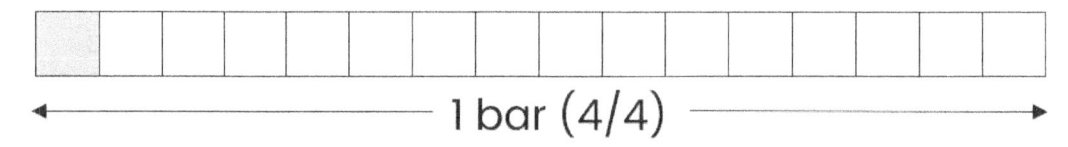

Figure 2.10: A sixteenth note within a bar of 4/4.

The five time values so far considered, the whole, half, quarter, eighth and sixteenth—are enough for most purposes. However, occasionally you are going to want to use even shorter time values.

Next in the hierarchy is the thirty-second note. They are represented by the symbol shown in Figure 2.11:

Figure 2.11: A thirty-second note.

On the piano roll, they appear as shown in Figure 2.12:

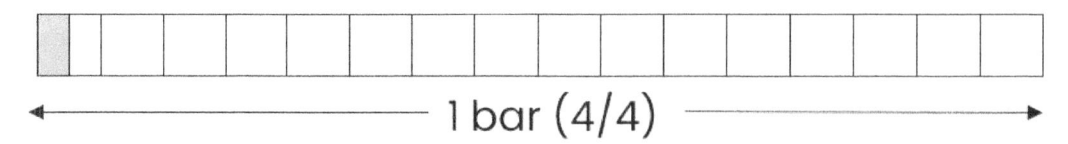

Figure 2.12: A thirty-second note within a bar of 4/4.

Finally, there are sixty-fourth notes, represented by the symbol in Figure 2.13:

Figure 2.13: A sixty-fourth note.

These appear in your DAW as shown in Figure 2.14:

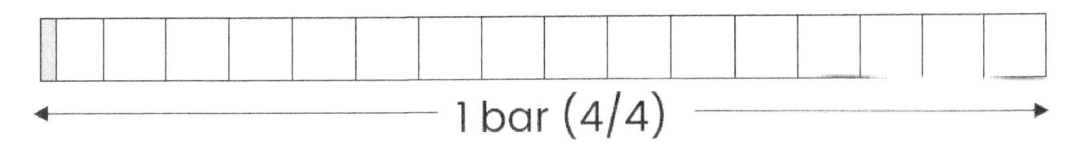

Figure 2.14: A sixty-fourth note within a bar of 4/4.

Thirty-second and sixty-fourth notes are far from redundant features brought over from the sphere of written music. In terms of modern styles, you will often hear them in styles such as trap music, punctuating the beat with short bursts of percussion. An example of this is shown In Figure 2.15:

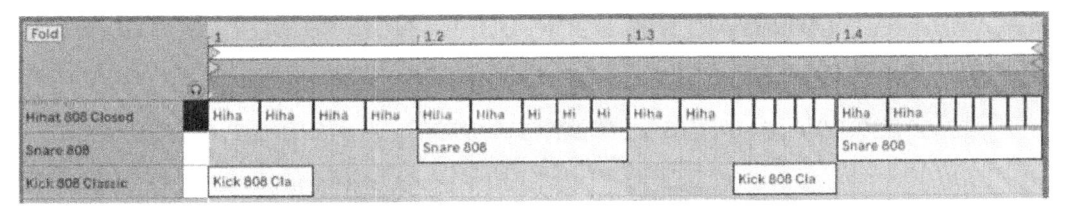

Figure 2.15: Thirty-second and sixty-fourth notes within a drum track.

We have set out seven levels of time values which, beginning with the whole note, allow for the definition of the duration of any musical event that we want. A helpful memory exercise is to consider the hierarchy of the notes in a note tree, as shown in Figure 2.16:

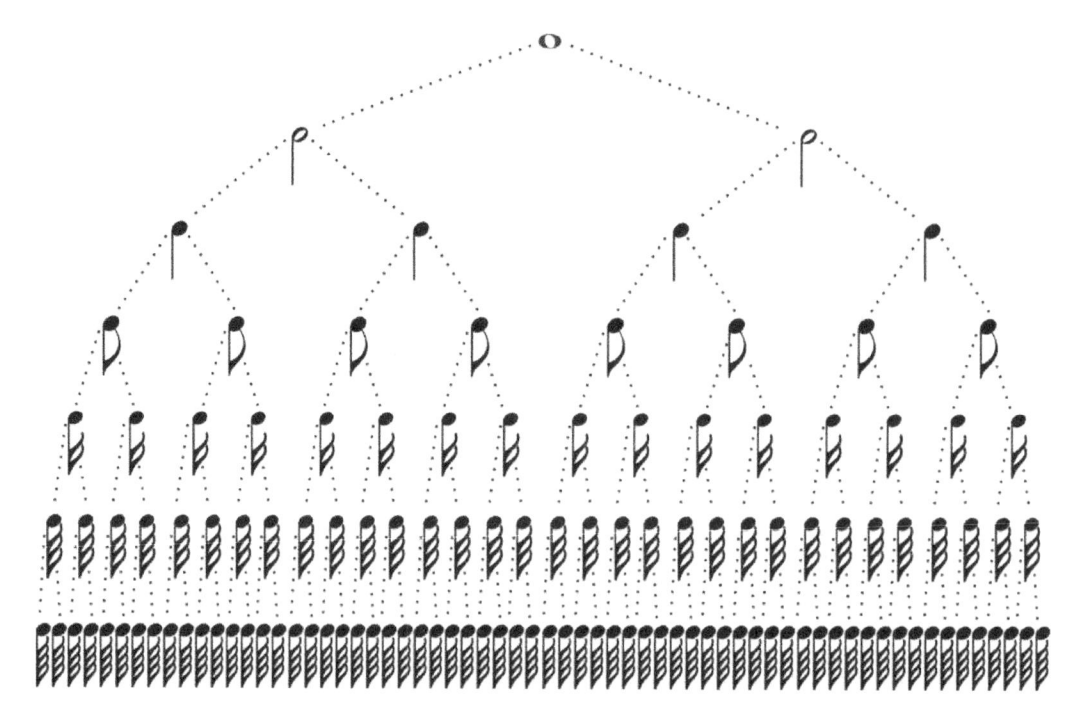

Figure 2.16: The note tree.

It's worth knowing that there are differences in nomenclature between British terminology and American terminology. I have used American terminology in this book, but for your reference, Table 2.1 displays both.

Table 2.1: Note values, their symbols, American terms and British terms.

Value	Symbol	American term	British term
1	o	Whole note	Semibreve
1/2	𝅗𝅥	Half note	Minim
1/4	♩	Quarter note	Crotchet
1/8	♪	Eighth note	Quaver
1/16	𝅘𝅥𝅯	Sixteenth note	Semiquaver
1/32	𝅘𝅥𝅰	Thirty-second note	Demisemiquaver
1/64	𝅘𝅥𝅱	Sixty-fourth note	Hemidemisemiquaver

Beaming

When looking at music in written form, you will commonly see note values being beamed together into groups. The beam is a horizontal bar that is placed over or under the notes that then joins them together. An example of one is shown in Figure 2.17:

♪ ♪ ♪ ♪   Group of four eighth notes

𝅘𝅥𝅮𝅘𝅥𝅮𝅘𝅥𝅮𝅘𝅥𝅮   Group of four eighth notes (beamed)

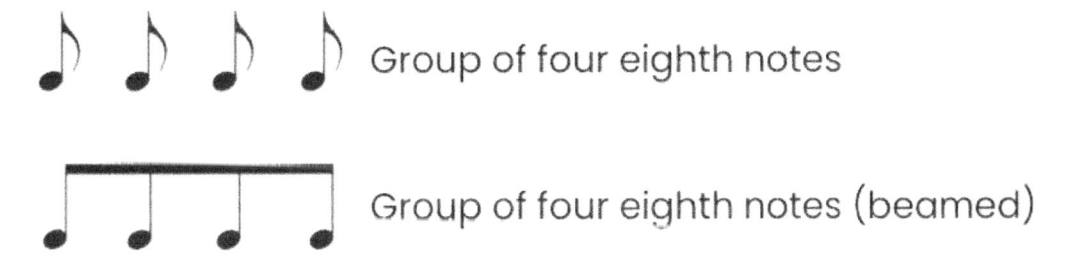

Figure 2.17: Two groups of four eighth notes, one beamed, the other not beamed.

Beams came into use when composers used to write scores by hand. They were used to show how notes should be grouped together according to the prevailing meter. They were also used as a matter of economy. Imagine writing out a succession of thirty-two thirty-second notes, each individual note of which would need three flags. Using beams, they can all be covered with a few simple bars across the top or bottom of the notes, as shown in Figure 2.18:

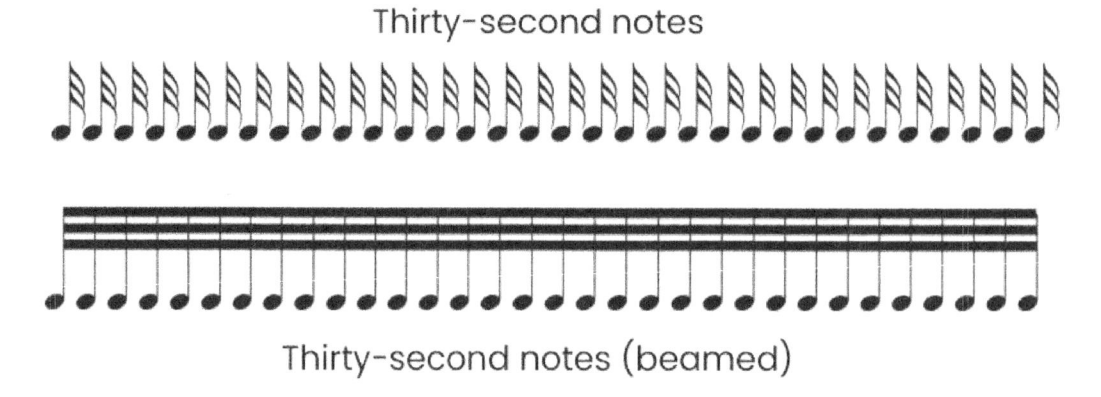

Figure 2.18: Two groups of thirty-two thirty-second notes, one not beamed, and the other beamed.

Another notational practise that you might come across is the use of dotted notes. A dot placed after a note value extends its value by a half. Therefore, for example, a dotted quarter note is equivalent to a quarter note plus half of a quarter note—which is an eighth note. Its value is equivalent to three eighths, as you can see in Figure 2.19:

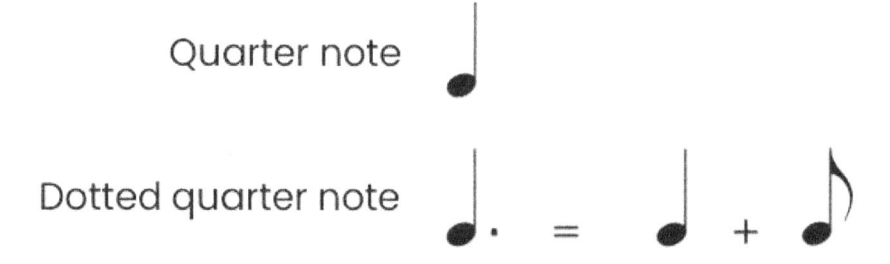

Figure 2.19: A dotted quarter note.

Accents

An accent is a method of articulating a note. When you see an accent symbol (>) above a note, it means that the note is to be played with emphasis. An example of this is displayed in Figure 2.20:

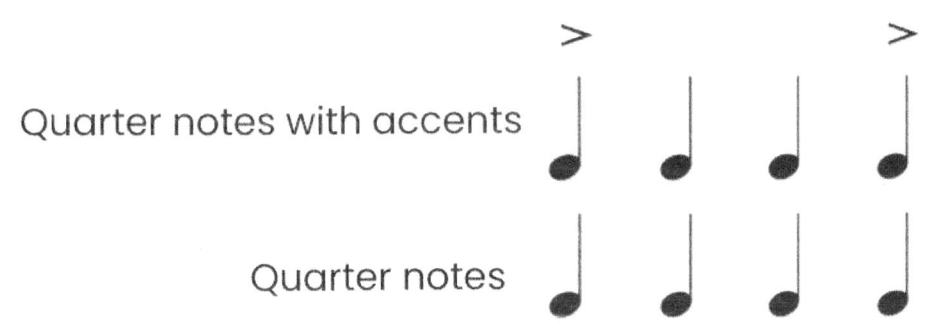

Figure 2.20: Accents on the first and last quarter notes of a bar.

As you'll discover later in the book, this is important for the study of meter.

Triplets

So far, the notes that we've seen work in divisions or multiplications of two.

Throughout the history of music, however, musicians and composers have also sought to divide beats up into three sub-beats. These are commonly called triplets. Figure 2.21, for example, is a typical rhythm that uses quarter and eighth notes:

Figure 2.21: A rhythm using quarter and eighth notes.

In this rhythm, however, the pairs of eighths have now been replaced by eighth triplets. In recognition of this, you will see, in Figure 2.22, a small three placed over the beamed eighth notes:

Figure 2.22: The pairs of eighths have become triplets.

What qualifies them as being triplets is that there are now three eighth notes at the same time as two. We shall delve into these in more depth later in the book, but in the meantime be aware that these are readily available in DAW software, being usually represented by the fraction 1/12.

Similarly, if you want to divide each eighth note into three sub-beats rather than two, you will then want twenty-fourths rather than sixteenths. The difference between two notes and three triplets within a grid is shown in Figure 2.23:

Two notes

Triplets

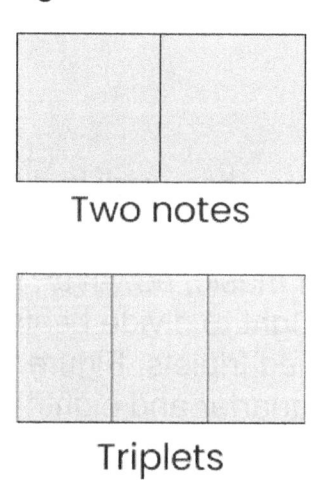

Figure 2.23: Triplets are three notes in the time of two.

When looking for these time values in the MIDI editor of your DAW, there are slight differences in how these time values are described. Table 2.2 shows you how they are named within three of the most popular DAWs: Ableton, Reason and Logic.

Table 2.2: How note values are termed within three popular DAWs.

Time value	Ableton	Reason	Logic
Whole note	1 Bar	Bar	1/1
Half note	1/2	1/2	1/2
Quarter note	1/4	1/4	1/4
Eighth note	1/8	1/8	1/8
Sixteenth note	1/16	1/16	1/16
Thirty second note	1/32	1/32	1/32
Sixty-fourth note	1/64	1/64	1/64
Eighth triplet	1/8 (Triplet grid activated)	1/8T	1/8 Triplet (1/12)
Sixteenth triplet	1/16 (Triplet grid activated)	1/16T	1/16 Triplet (1/24)

So, we have seen that time values used for the expression of the duration of musical events begin with the premise of the whole note. The whole note is thereafter divided up into various fractions of that whole. These, in their turn, then enable the producer to express the duration of musical events precisely.

Exercises

Recall the fractional names (i.e., whole note, half note, etc.) of the following note values:

1) How many:
   a) eighth notes are there in a half note?
   b) sixteenth notes in a quarter note?
   c) whole notes are equivalent to thirty-two sixteenth notes?
   d) sixty-fourth notes in a half note?
   e) eighth notes are equivalent to sixty-four thirty-second notes?

2) Recall the name of the note value that represents the sum of all the values:

𝅗𝅥 + 𝅗𝅥 = ...

♪ + ♪ + ♪ + ♪ = ...

𝅘𝅥𝅯 + 𝅘𝅥𝅯 = ...

𝅘𝅥𝅰 + 𝅘𝅥𝅰 + 𝅘𝅥𝅰 + 𝅘𝅥𝅰 + 𝅘𝅥𝅰 + 𝅘𝅥𝅰 + 𝅘𝅥𝅰 = ...

♩ + ♩ + ♩ + ♩ = ...

CHAPTER 3: TIME SIGNATURES

The beats and time values we've discussed need grouping into a sensible structure. This is accomplished through a **time signature**. An example of one is shown in Figure 3.1:

4/4

Figure 3.1: A 4/4 time signature in Reason.

The time signature represents an exact measurement of the length of each bar of music. It comprises two numbers, written rather like a fraction.

The first number is called the *numerator,* and this tells you how many beats there are in a single bar of the music. Our DAWs offer us a default setting for this, which is 4. This tells us that our DAW will offer us four beats per bar of the music.

The second number is the *denominator*, and this tells you the time value of each beat. Here, we can see the number 4, which signifies the value of a quarter note. 4/4 therefore signifies a measure of four quarter notes per bar. This is shown in Figure 3.2:

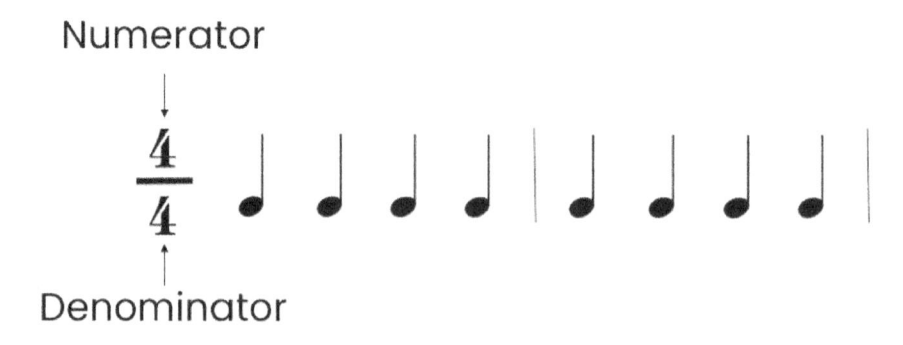

Figure 3.2: Four quarter notes per bar in a 4/4 time signature.

Both the upper and the lower number can be changed in a time signature. Each such change will produce a different measure per bar. So, for example, we could change the denominator to 8. What this means is that each bar will comprise four eighth note steps, as shown in Figure 3.3:

Figure 3.3: Four eighth notes per bar in a 4/8 time signature.

Alternatively, we could set the numerator to 7, for example, producing a time signature of 7/8. This would signify a bar comprising seven eighth note steps per bar, as you can see in Figure 3.4:

Figure 3.4: Seven quarter notes per bar in a 7/8 time signature.

For some contemporary music producers, time signatures aren't often given much thought. That's because they are often content to work within 4/4 as the default time signature.

However, 4/4 is just one of many time signatures. And while there is clearly a great deal of music yet to be written in 4/4 time, some of the most innovative music is produced outside of the box of 4/4.

For example, *Get Centred* by Joe is a piece of tribal house that defies the conventions of that genre by being written in 7/8. Similarly, Radiohead's masterpiece *Everything in its Right Place* implies a time signature of 10/4.

Many of the most innovative musicians look outside of the constraints of 4/4 when seeking inspiration. With this in mind, let's now see how time signatures work. Figure 3.5 below shows a DAW grid set to a resolution of sixteenths for a single bar of a drum track that uses 4/4:

Figure 3.5: A bar of 4/4 within Ableton Live.

Now, let's explore some alternative time signatures and see how the grid then changes in response. Let's start with the time signature used by Joe in *Get Lifted,* which is 7/8, shown in Figure 3.6:

Figure 3.6: A bar of 7/8 in Ableton Live.

As you can see, a single bar now has seven beats, and each beat has a value of one eighth.

Now let's look at Figure 3.7, showing 10/4, as used by Radiohead:

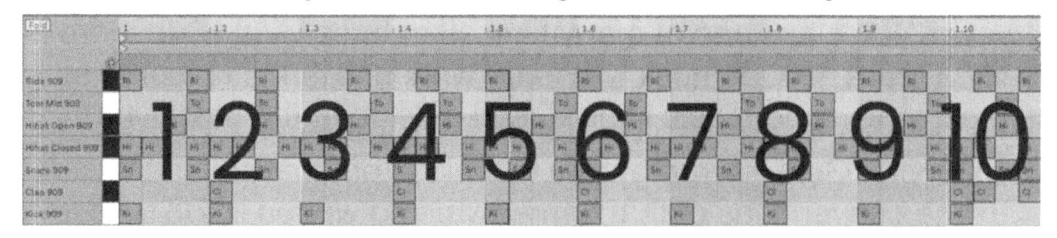

Figure 3.7: A bar of 10/4 in Ableton Live.

As you can see, a single bar now has ten beats—but in this case, each beat has a value of a quarter note.

Using time signatures, we can write music whose bars comprise any number of steps, each of which will have its own set time value.

Remember, the top number, the numerator, shows how many steps there are per bar; while the bottom number, the denominator, shows the time value of those steps. So, can you answer these questions?

1. What does a time signature of 3/4 indicate?
2. What does a time signature of 11/8 indicate?
3. What does a time signature of 7/16 indicate?

If you can answer these questions, then you understand what a time signature is.

Your DAW software should adapt to time signature changes. For example, in Ableton, if you change the time signature to 3/4 in the top-left of the screen, as shown in Figure 3.8:

Figure 3.8: The time signature within Ableton Live (centre).

You will notice your clips adapt to this change, showing three beats to the bar, as seen in Figure 3.9:

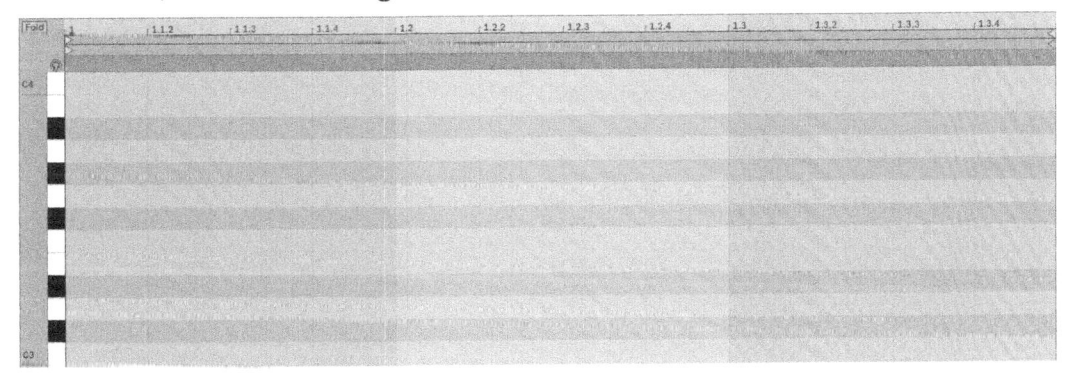

Figure 3.9: A MIDI clip within Ableton Live after the time signature has been changed to 3/4.

As each beat is a quarter note, this means that a bar will now comprise six eighth note steps, twelve sixteenth note steps or twenty-four thirty-second note steps. For you, perhaps used to the default time signature of 4/4, this might be a novel way of structuring time within your work.

Exercises
1. Try writing a drum track in a 3/4 time signature.
2. Try writing a melody in a 7/8 time signature.

CHAPTER 4: METER

We've looked at time signatures, which tell us the duration of the musical beats, and how any of them there are per bar. These bars are merely the storage medium for the music itself. The music itself is governed by a concept called **meter**.

Meter is a temporal framework that organises the pulse stream into a series of beat patterns that then give a sense of order and shape to the rhythm of the music. Using such patterns is universal: wherever in the world music is practised and played, you will find the use of meter.

Several features are common to the use of metric patterns. The first is the concept of a metric cycle. Like its name suggests, this is a repeating cycle comprising so many beats or steps. Each cycle is equivalent to a single bar or measure of the music. Once that cycle has completed, it may then begin again and—if the meter of the music remains unchanged—subsequently repeat itself cyclically for the duration of the entire piece of music.

When studying meter, it is useful to think of a metric pattern as being like a wheel that is turning over and over. Each turn of the wheel is equivalent to a single bar of the music. In Figure 4.1, we can see a metric cycle has four beats or steps to the bar.

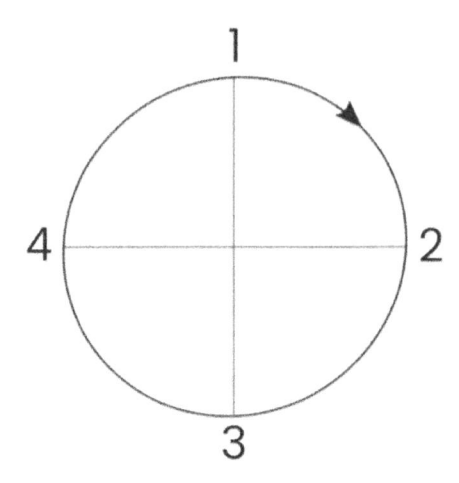

Figure 4.1: Four beats to the bar expressed as a cycle.

Another feature common to the use of metric patterns is a stress to emphasise certain beats of the metric cycle. This stress can be a louder note, a fundamental note in a scale, or even a note from an instrument of brighter timbre. The most important thing is that this stress is used to tell the listener that an emphasis is happening.

Inevitably, the most powerful stress is placed on the first beat of the bar, for it is this that announces to the listener the commencement of a new metric cycle. Other beats of the bar can receive stress, but it is usually less than the stress of the first beat:

One, two, three, four, **one,** two, three, four.

As you will soon discover, each meter implies a certain hierarchy of beats and sub-beats. Aware of this, musicians can use stresses to either support that beat hierarchy, or sometimes, challenge or subvert it.

To learn about the use of meter in music, it is useful to study a model of meter that not only works, but that has a proven track record for modern music producers.

One such model is the Western system of musical meter, that in one form or another, has dominated Western music for at least the last

300 years. As this system represents a great place to begin our study of meter, let us now consider the basic elements of that system, the musical logic behind it and, of course, how to use that system within our music.

First, to the system itself.

In the classical system of meter, there are two kinds of meter, which are termed *simple* and *compound*. Each of these then breaks down into a further three kinds, which are *duple, triple* and *quadruple*. This means that there are six basic metric patterns:

1. Simple duple
2. Compound duple
3. Simple triple
4. Compound triple
5. Simple quadruple
6. Compound quadruple

When studying this system, the first point to address is the distinction between simple and compound meter. This comes down to how the meter divides the basic beat. In *simple meter*, the beat breaks down into **pairs** of sub-beats. Two quarter notes will break down into four eighth notes, which in their turn will break down into eight sixteenth notes and so on.

In *compound meter*, the beat breaks down into **three** sub-beats. Two quarter notes will break down into six eighth notes, which will break down into twelve sixteenth notes and so on. This is illustrated in Figure 4.2:

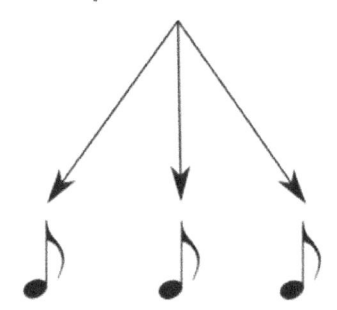

Figure 4.2: Simple meter breaks down into two sub-beats, whereas compound meter breaks down into three.

This difference in the grouping of sub-beats affects the overall feel and flow of the meter. Compound meters have a different feel to simple meters, the groups of three sub-beats giving them a certain lilt that will be readily discernible to a listener.

The terms duple, triple and quadruple refer to the number of main beats in the bar. Duple meter is a meter in which there are two main beats to the bar. In triple meter, there are three main beats to the bar, while in quadruple meter, there are four main beats to the bar.

Be aware that when studying meter, the terms *meter* and *time* can be used interchangeably—so *simple duple meter* and *simple duple time* mean the same thing. With that said, let's get started!

Duple, Triple and Quadruple Meter

Now that we have understood the terms of the system, let us now consider each of the six classical metric patterns.

Simple Meter

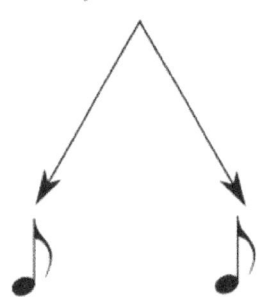

In this section, we will analyse the three metric patterns that are classed as forms of simple time.

These are:
- Simple duple meter
- Simple triple meter
- Simple quadruple meter

Simple meter means that the main beats will break down into pairs.

Simple Duple Meter

The unit of measure for a metric pattern is represented by the beat (or step). A complete metric cycle, containing more than one beat, is represented by the bar. You can see this in your DAW, in which musical time is divided up into successive bars.

There are two beats per bar in simple duple meter. Because of this, the numerator of the time signature will have a value of 2. The value of the denominator can, of course, vary, depending upon the note value that you have chosen to represent the beat. If the beat is a half note, the time signature will be 2/2, while if the beat is a quarter note, the time signature will be 2/4, etc. You can see this in Figure 4.3:

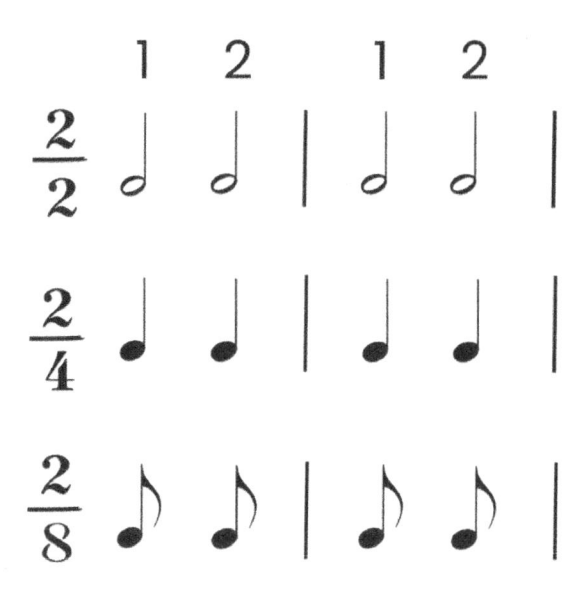

Figure 4.3: Simple duple meter always has two beats to the bar.

When you work with duple meter, you soon realise that it represents one of the most natural metric patterns that it is possible to use. This is because its two-step rhythm is reflected in many natural processes. Consider, for example, the basic rhythm of walking, which is essentially a two-step pattern:

Left, right, left, right.

Comprising one beat—the antecedent—followed by another—the consequent, simple duple meter presents the music producer with a consistent, predictable, continually repeating two-step pattern.

Let's now consider the term 'simple' and what that means. Simple time means that each of the duple meter's two steps will break down into pairs. This breakdown creates a growing hierarchy of beats in which 1—the unit of the bar—divides into two quarter note steps. Those two quarter note steps, in their turn, break down into two eighth notes and so on. Figure 4.4 will reveal this temporal hierarchy and the rhythmic environment that it generates:

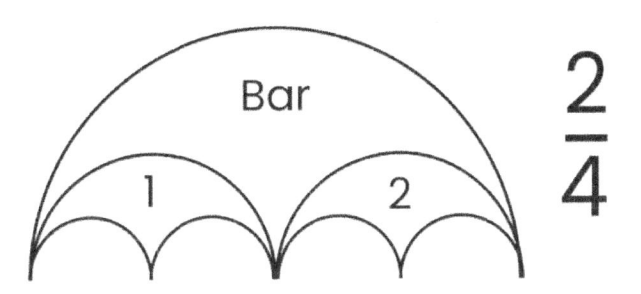

Figure 4.4: The hierarchy of simple duple meter means each unit breaks down into two.

Contemporary examples of simple duple meter include:
- Queen's *We Will Rock You*
- Massivo Attack's *Teardrop*
- Drexciya's *Under Sea Disturbances*
- Joy Division's *Love Will Tear Us Apart*
- Smith N Hack's *Falling Stars*

Simple duple meter has a long history of usage behind it. Indeed, it is and has been fundamental to many styles of music. Try counting along with the music to appreciate the qualities of simple duple meter.

In contemporary music, duple meter is rarely reflected by the time signature. This is because two bars of 2/4 fit perfectly into one bar of 4/4. Therefore, there is not a great deal of point changing the time signature from 4/4 to 2/4. After all, what producers often want is the *feel* that duple meter gives to their music. How the music appears in their DAW is therefore somewhat irrelevant.

This draws us to an important point—it's easy to confuse meter with time signature. Remember that the time signature only tells you how many beats there are per bar, and what time value those beats are. Meter, on the other hand, is the rhythmic framework that guides your music.

Writing in simple duple meter doesn't mean you have to have a beat on one and two—in Figure 4.5, you'll see a motif develop from its simplest possibility into something more complex. Try playing each of these motifs. You could do so by clapping your hands, or by tapping your fingers on a table.

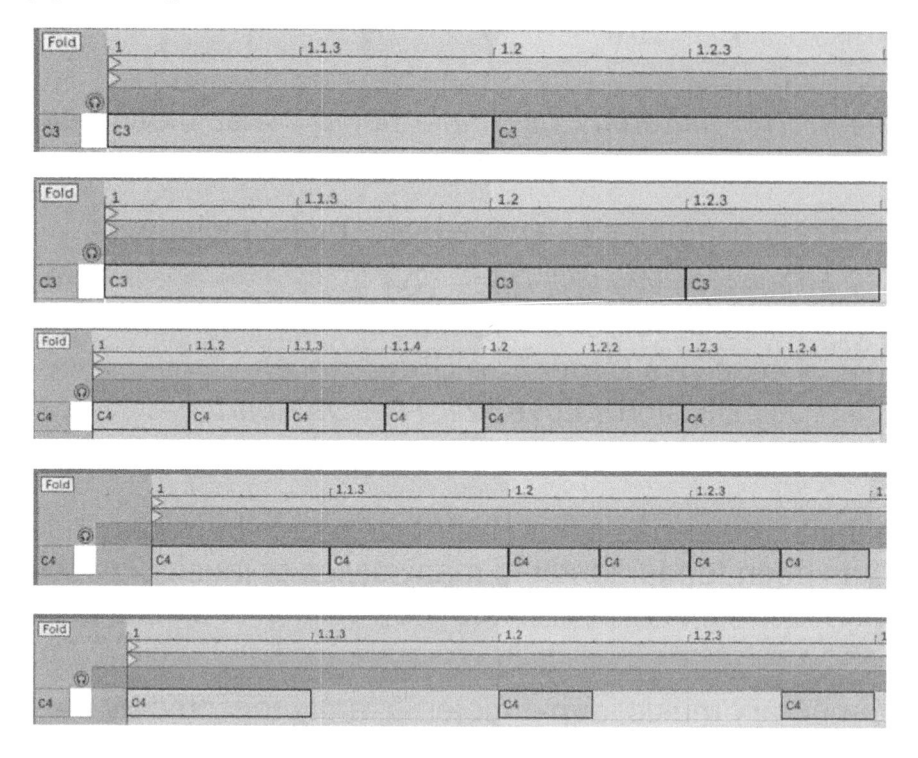

Figure 4.5: A motif developing from its simplest possible iteration into something more complex.

Between note values and their equivalent rests, it is possible to create an infinite variety of interesting rhythms within the framework of a meter. If the sum of the note values and their rests adds up to a pattern of two equal beats, you are working in duple meter.

Having considered simple duple meter, let's move on to simple triple meter.

Simple Triple Meter

Simple triple meter has three beats to the bar (as opposed to the two in simple duple meter). This number of beats is naturally reflected by the time signatures chosen for the use of triple meter. These do and can include those shown in Figure 4.6:

Figure 4.6: Within simple triple meter, there are three main beats.

Notice that the key feature of the time signature is the numerator, which, for simple triple meter, is always 3.

When trying to understand any kind of meter, it is vital to consider the different levels of temporal organisation that define it.

First, there is the level of the entire bar, which amounts to one complete metric cycle. As you can see in Figure 4.7, this has a length of three quarter notes.

Second is the level of the main beat, each of which can be assigned a number from one through to three.

Third is the level of the sub-beat. Being simple time, note that each of the main beats break down into pairs.

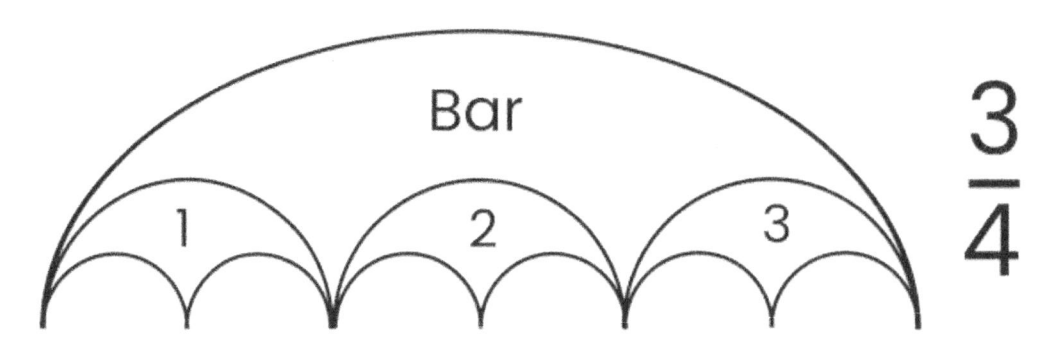

Figure 4.7: Simple triple meter's three beats break down into groups of two sub-beats.

Notice how the rhythmic environment of triple meter is being defined by a different set of numbers. The keys to it are 1, 3 and 6. To appreciate what this means, spend some time getting to know and developing a feel for the use simple triple meter. A good way to do this is to count the beats out loud, assigning to each a number.

One, two, three, **one**, two, three, etc.

As you do so, allow your head to nod with the count. You will soon get a sense of the uniqueness of simple triple meter.

Simple triple meter is not heard in contemporary music often, but examples include:

- *Stay Tuned* by Gang Starr
- *The Only Mistake* by Joy Division
- *Tears* by Sterac

Now that we understand simple triple meter, let's have a look at simple quadruple meter.

Simple Quadruple Meter

Quadruple meter is where there are four beats in a bar, with the emphasis on the first and a smaller emphasis on the third.

Simple quadruple meter's hierarchy evolves in multiples and divisors of four: 1, 4 and 8 being the principle numbers involved, as shown in Figure 4.8:

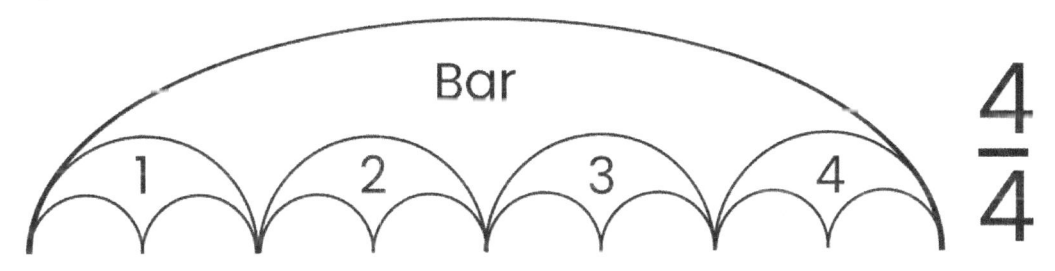

Figure 4.8: Simple quadruple meter's four main beats break down into eight sub-beats.

Simple quadruple meter represents a staple for music that has endured for hundreds of years. You'll know it from the typical way it's counted: ONE, two, *three,* four. In fact, it is often referred to as 'common time' in recognition of this.

Much of modern pop and electronic music is written in simple quadruple time. Examples include:

- Peggy Gou's *Han Jan*
- Mala's *Lean Forward*
- Origin Unknown's *Valley Of the Shadows*

You may wonder what the difference is between duple meter and quadruple meter. If a single bar of quadruple meter divides into two bars of duple meter and two bars of duple meter fit into a single bar of quadruple meter, what's the difference?

Back in the days of music written on a staff, it would be easy to differentiate between the two. Music in duple time would have 2 as the numerator within the time signature, whereas music in quadruple time would have 4 as the numerator.

Now that music is written in DAWs, mostly in the default of 4/4, it can be harder to tell the two apart. The answer here lies within the **emphasis**. You can create a duple meter rhythm by repeating the word 'water' at a medium pace—

'wa-ter, wa-ter, wa-ter.'

Whereas, a quadruple meter can be created by repeating the word 'distribution'—

'di-stri-bu-tion, di-stri-bu-tion, di-stri-bu-tion.'

Let's compare the two meters using actual music.

Listen to *Minus* by Robert Hood. You can tell that this is in duple meter by the balance of the primary and secondary beats.

By comparison, listen to *M04.5a* by Maurizio. This is in quadruple meter—you can hear a major emphasis on the first beat, followed by a minor emphasis on the third.

These may seem like academic considerations, but once you get creative and start moving the emphases around, you'll find that both frameworks have a distinct identity.

Now that we have considered the three simple meters, in the next section we are going to look at their alternative forms as they appear under the guise of *compound meter*.

Compound Meter

In the last section, we looked at simple meter, whether duple, triple, or quadruple. In this section, we're going to study compound meter, which also has within it the three divisions of duple, triple and quadruple. Having done so, we will be familiar with the metric system that has prevailed within the world of classical music for over 300 years.

While in simple meter each beat breaks down into a pair of sub-beats, in compound meter, each beat breaks down into three-sub-beats, rather than two. This is seen in Figure 4.9:

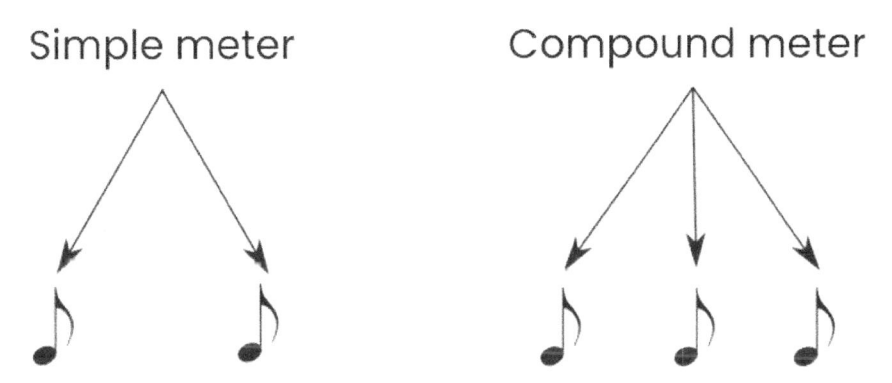

Figure 4.9: Whereas the beats in simple meter break down into two sub-beats, the beats of compound meter break down into three sub-beats.

The result is a group of metric patterns that offer a major contrast to the patterns of simple meter. With this in mind, let's review compound meters, starting with compound duple meter.

Compound Duple Meter

In compound duple meter, the main beats (1 and 2) break down into three sub-beats each. This produces a bar comprising two groups of three beats each, as shown in Figure 4.10:

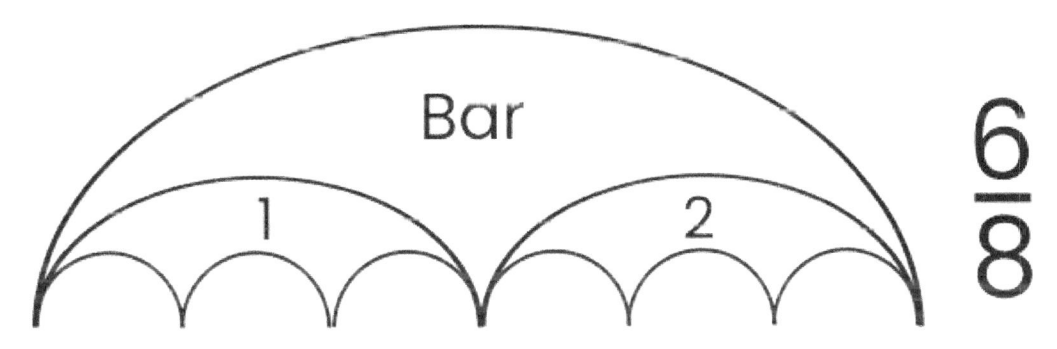

Figure 4.10: The two beats of compound duple meter break down into six sub-beats in total.

Mathematically, this generates a rhythmic environment defined by the numbers 1, 2, and 6.

The top layer is the level of the bar, while the level below that represents the main beats 1 and 2. The third level shows the division of those beats into threes. This is the essence of compound duple meter. Like simple duple meter, it is a two-step pattern, the difference lying in the breakdown of each step into three sub-beats.

When studying compound time, you'll come across an illogicality: in simple time, the numerator of the time signature tells you how many beats there are in a bar. Whereas, in compound time, the numerator really tells you how many sub-beats there are in a bar.

Because of this, the numerator of the time signature for compound duple time is **6**, comprising two groups of three sub-beats each. The denominator can of course, vary—all depending upon which note value is used to express the main beat. So, a time signature of 6/4 means that there are six quarter note beats in the bar. A time signature of 6/16 will mean that there are six sixteenth note beats in the bar. This is illustrated in Figure 4.11:

Figure 4.11: The numerator of compound duple meter is 6.

To get a grasp of compound duple meter, count it. One way you could do this is by counting the following pattern out loud:

One, and, and, *two*, and, and.

This will get you used to using two groups of three in the bar.

Another way of counting is from one through to six placing an emphasis on beats one and four. When counting, place a particular emphasis on beat one as the first beat of the bar:

One, two, three, *four*, five, six.

This will get you familiar with the pattern of stresses that is typical of compound duple meter.

Compound duple was always popular during the era of Western classical music. Some excellent examples are:

- Beethoven's *Pastoral Symphony*
- Morning Mood from the Peer Gynt Suite by Grieg

- Offenbach—the Barcarolle from Tales of Hoffman

A miscellany of contemporary songs use it, including:
- *I Can't Help* by Elvis Presley
- *Call Me* by Blondie
- *Nothing Else Matters* by Metallica
- Leftfield's *6/8 War*
- *Gratis* by Thomas Fehlmann.

As you can hear, compound duple meter's characteristic swinging rhythm creates a contrast to simple duple meter. To illustrate the difference between simple and compound duple meter, let's look at a basic House drum beat on a DAW grid. Figure 4.12 shows the beat in simple duple meter:

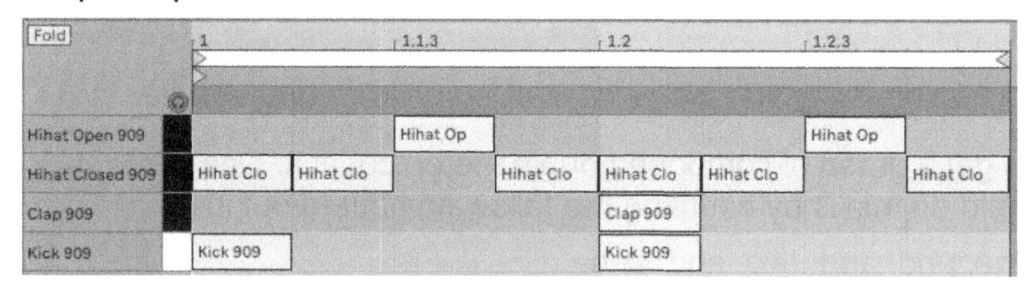

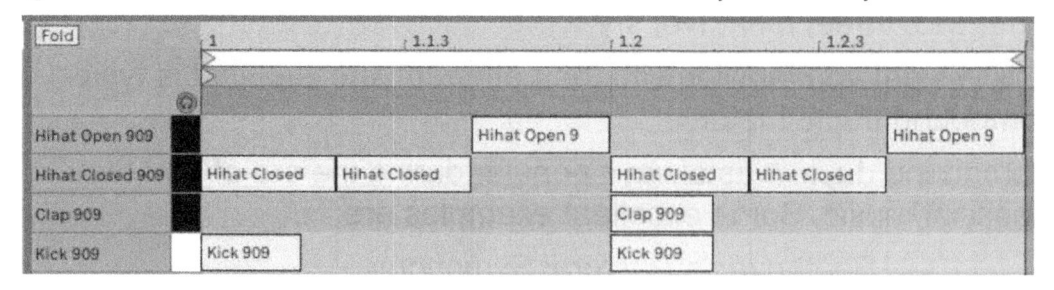

Figure 4.12: A beat in Ableton's grid, written in simple duple meter.

Notice how the open hi-hat sits precisely halfway through the beat. Figure 4.13 shows the same drum beat in compound duple time:

Figure 4.13: A beat in Ableton's grid, written in compound duple meter.

Notice how the open hi-hat now sits two-thirds through the beat. This creates an asymmetric, off-balance feel.

Compound duple meter is commonly written in DAW software by setting the time signature to 6/8. However, it could also be written in 2/4 by manually changing the grid settings to triplets. An example of doing this in Ableton Live is shown in Figure 4.14.

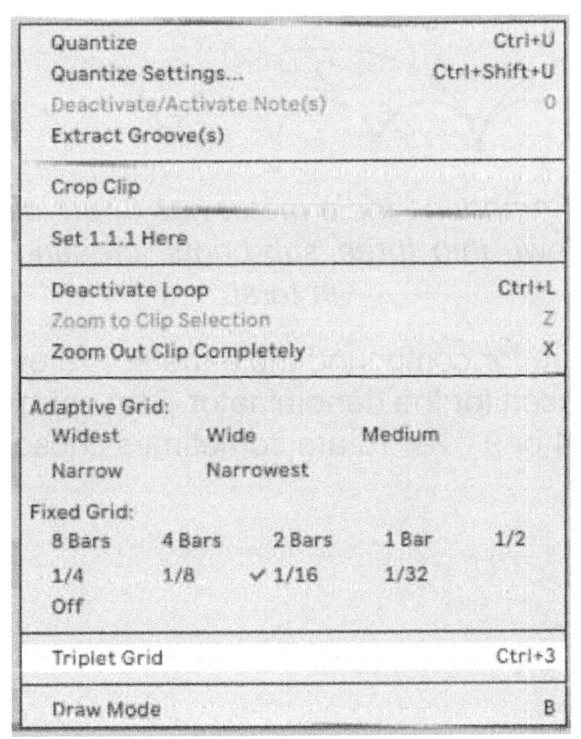

Figure 4.14: Activating Triplet Grid in Ableton Live.

This is useful if you wish to switch between simple and compound duple meter—or even combining the two (but we'll get to that later!).

Now that we have considered compound duple time, let us now look at compound triple meter.

Compound Triple Meter

In compound triple meter, each of the three main beats breaks down into a further three sub-beats, totalling nine in all. This gives compound triple meter the characteristic expression of three groups of three beats each, as shown in Figure 4.15:

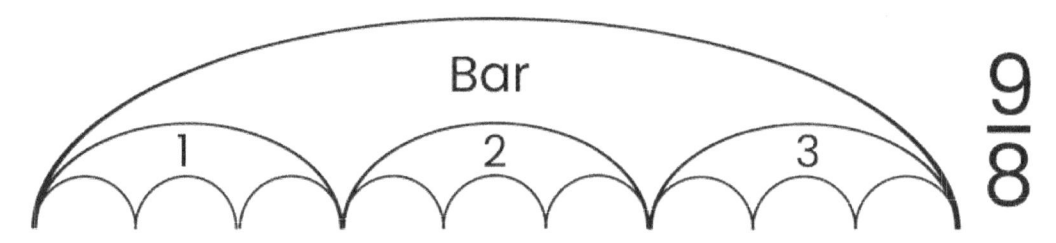

Figure 4.15: Compound triple meter has three beats, each of which break down into three sub-beats, creating nine sub-beats in total.

The time signature for compound triple meter is 9 over whatever note value is chosen for the denominator. The norm is 9 over 8, however 9 over 4 or 9 over 16 are sometimes chosen, as shown in Figure 4.16:

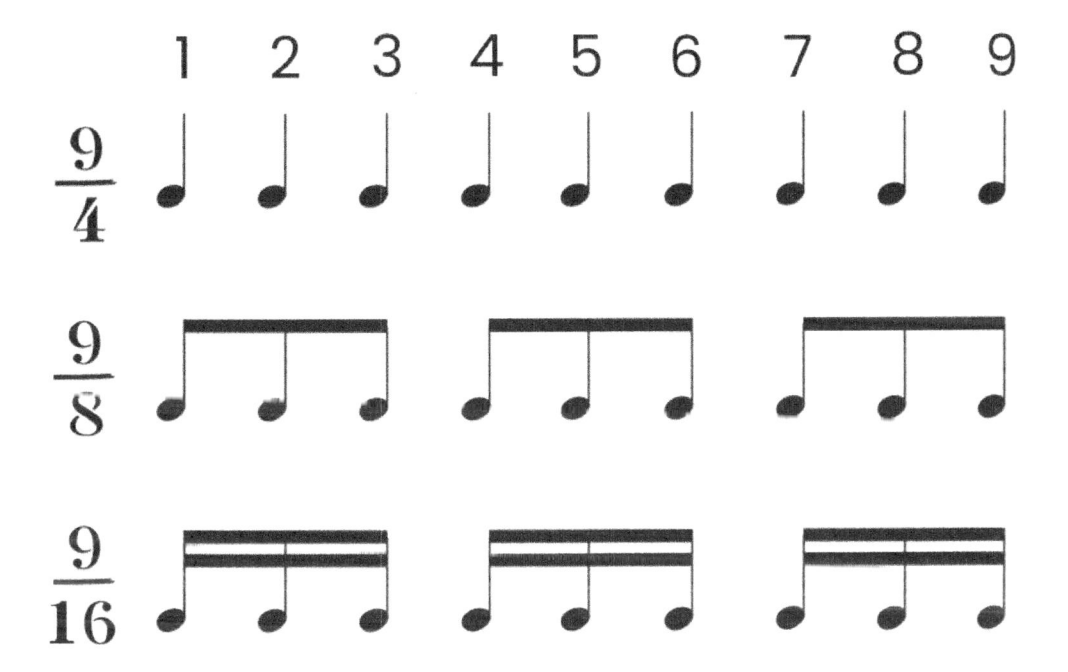

Figure 4.16: the numerator in compound triple meter is 9.

Triple compound meter is possibly the least-used meter in contemporary music—so much so that you may find it takes a while for your ears to adjust to it.

To me, this would therefore suggest that if you like pushing the envelope of music, compound triple meter is a great opportunity to do so. To encourage you, here is some music that you can listen to that uses compound triple meter:

- *Blue Ronda A La Turk* by Dave Brubeck
- *Jesu, Joy Of Man's Desire* by Bach
- *Clair de Lune* by Debussy
- *Ride Of The Valkyries* by Wagner

Figure 4.17 below shows an example of a drum track written in compound triple meter. Notice how each of the three main beats is divided into three sub-beats:

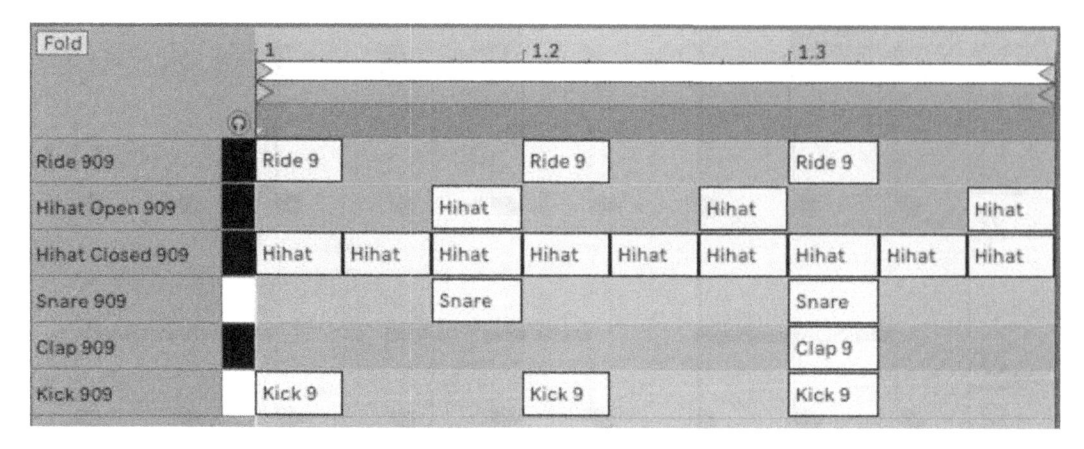

Figure 4.17: a drum beat in Ableton's grid, written in compound triple meter.

To count in compound triple meter, count to nine, with emphases on one, four and seven, laying a particular emphasis on beat one as the first beat of the bar:

One, two, three, *four*, five, six, *seven*, eight, nine.

Alternatively, try:

One, and, and, *two,* and, and, *three,* and, and.

Compound triple meter leads us to our final meter: *compound quadruple meter.*

Compound quadruple meter

Compound quadruple meter has four main beats to the bar, each of which breaks down into three sub-beats. This produces four groups of three sub-beats to the bar, totalling twelve, as shown in Figure 4.18:

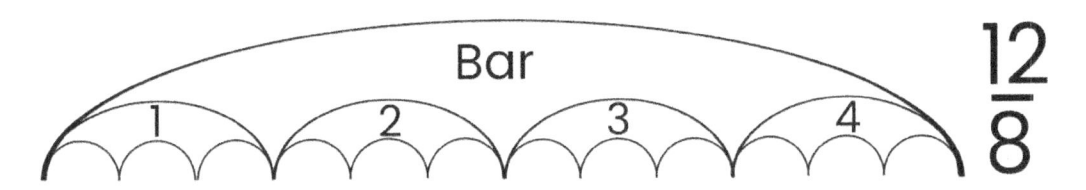

Figure 4.18: Compound quadruple meter's four beats break down into three sub-beats each, creating twelve sib-beats in total.

To show compound quadruple meter, we thus use a numerator of 12. The denominator can be any note value that we choose to be the rhythmic unit, although 8 is most commonly used. This is shown in Figure 4.19:

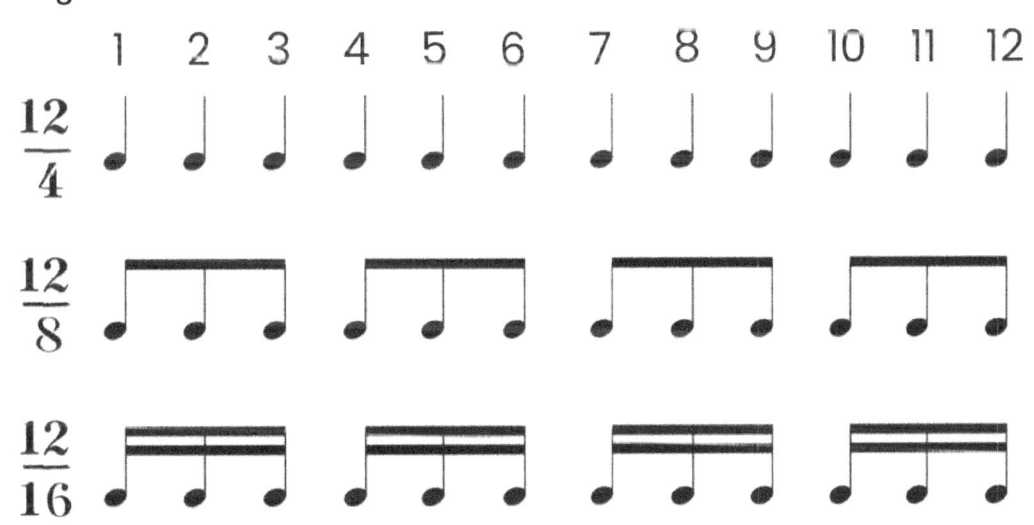

Figure 4.19: The numerator in compound quadruple meter is 12.

Whatever the denominator, the characteristic breakdown of the four beats into three sub-beats represents the defining feature of compound quadruple time.

Music producers will feel comfortable working in compound quadruple time. This is because it has four beats to the bar. The only difference between compound quadruple and the regular 4/4 is the fact that the beats are breaking down into threes. To get a sense of this, try counting in compound quadruple meter, placing an accent upon the first of each group of three. In doing so, remember to put a strong accent on the first beat of each bar to announce the beginning of the metric cycle:

One, two, three, *four,* five, six, *seven,* eight, nine, *ten,* eleven, twelve.

When you work with compound quadruple time, you realise that compared to simple quadruple time, it has a swinging quality, which has always made it popular. In this respect, it often appears with the second beat of each group of three missed out.

When we take compound quadruple time into the DAW, we can see that even though, traditionally, compound quadruple meter uses 12 as the numerator, it is easier to program compound quadruple meter into a DAW by setting the time signature as 4/4 and selecting Triplets using the grid. This is not necessarily because you are writing triplets, this is simply an expedient way to enter three sub-beats into your piano roll.

Contemporary songs that harness compound quadruple time include:

- *I Can't Help Falling in Love* by Elvis Presley
- *Black Skinhead* by Kanye West
- *Higher Ground* by Stevie Wonder
- *4 Leaf Clover* by Erykah Badu
- *Everybody Wants To Rule The World* by Tears for Fears

Recap

Once you've gained some experience in using simple and compound time—of whatever numeration—two, three or four, a world of metric possibility will emerge. I believe compound meters are underutilised by contemporary music producers, particularly those writing electronic music.

There is a vital symbiotic relationship between meter and rhythm. Rhythm benefits from the structured form of the meter, while meter benefits from the variations and creativity of rhythm. The result is a balance between structured form and free energy that is a delight to work with.

Exercises

1. Write a drum track in simple quadruple meter. Use perhaps 4-5 elements of the drum kit: a kick, snare, bass, hi-hat and cymbal.
2. Convert this drum track to compound quadruple meter.
3. Write a melodic loop in compound triple meter (9/8).

CHAPTER 5: IRREGULAR METER

The classical system of musical meter offers a good grounding in using metric patterns to bring order, regularity and precision to the rhythm of one's music. Being repetitive, these patterns help to develop a sense of rhythmic momentum that is featured in many types of music.

The classical system of meter also offers a bridge towards a more expansive, inventive use of meter, one that does not restrict itself to the constant use of four beats to the bar.

Logically, there is no good reason that most of the music tracks we create are written in quadruple meter. Electronic music—which we might think of as representing a bastion of musical freedom and experimentation, is, in fact, very conservative in its use of meter. In fact, it is almost as if there is an unconscious rule of four in place.

Running against this unconscious rule of four is the recognition among many music producers that for our music to continue to progress, develop and expand, there is ample room for experimentation with a wider variety of metric patterns. Towards this end, if you are accustomed to writing your music in quadruple meter, put aside some time to experiment with the use of these. You will find that metric patterns that go beyond the ubiquitous 4/4 have their own distinct qualities and appeal.

Breaking the Mould

Irregular or asymmetric meters are a relatively unexplored frontier in contemporary music, only being heard regularly in genres like IDM or math rock.

The main defining feature of these meters is that they have numerators—numbers of beats per bar—that do not fit in with the classical system of meter. To appreciate this, let's look at the number of beats per bar of the six classical meters within a number sequence:

1, **2, 3, 4,** 5, **6,** 7, 8, **9,** 10, 11, **12,** 13, 14, 15

Note that meters that have 5, 7, 10, 11, 13 or more beats to the bar are not used within the classical meter system.

Aware of this omission, Western classical composers, at least since the beginnings of the twentieth century, and sometimes before that, experimented with the use of these rather irregular types of meter. Their efforts to do this were largely inspired by the influence of other types of music on the Western tradition.

A good example of this is Eastern European folk music, where we will find many examples of the use of these irregular meters. They are also commonly used in Indian classical music and Turkish and Arabic musical styles. Their use today thoroughly enriches the spheres of musical composition and production.

Let's examine some of these irregular metric patterns, beginning with a meter that has five beats to the bar, which is called quintuple meter.

Quintuple Meter

Quintuple meter is a metric cycle in which there are five main beats to the bar. Using quintuple meter has a significant history going back even as far as ancient Greece. And since then, it has been used in many pieces of music, both Western and non-Western.

For simple quintuple time we use a numerator of five, the denominator of which can vary depending upon the note value that you choose to represent the beat. Figure 5.1 shows time signatures you might use when writing music in simple quintuple meter.

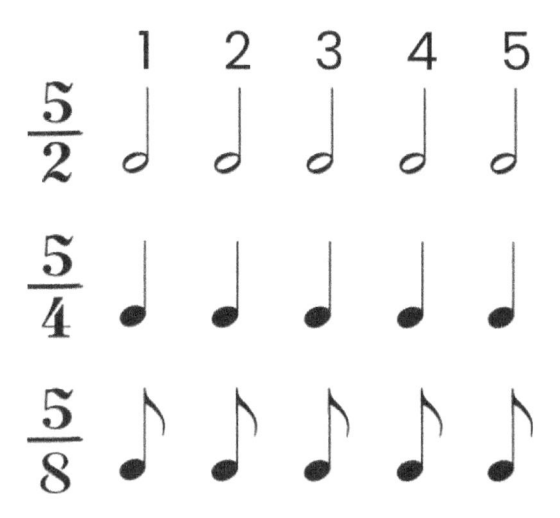

Figure 5.1: Quintuple meter has a numerator of 5.

As with the regular meters, there can also be a compound form of quintuple time, which then has fifteen beats to the bar, manifesting as five groups of three sub-beats, as shown in Figure 5.2:

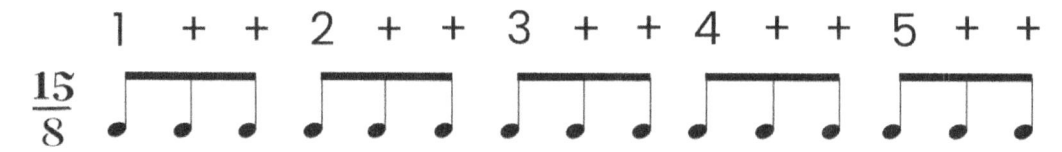

Figure 5.2: Compound quintuple meter's five beats break down into three sub-beats each, creating fifteen sub-beats in total.

To someone who is accustomed to hearing music that uses four beats to the bar, quintuple time can sound like a cycle of 4 + 1 beats to the bar, which can give the meter a curious, unsettling quality. However, rather than thinking of the grouping of beats in quintuple meter as comprising four plus one, try to think of it as being grouped into three and two, these two groups occurring in any order.

A good example of this is the theme from *Mission Impossible* by Lalo Schifrin. This is an easy and intuitive melody to listen to and sing, yet its meter is quintuple time (i.e. five beats to the bar):

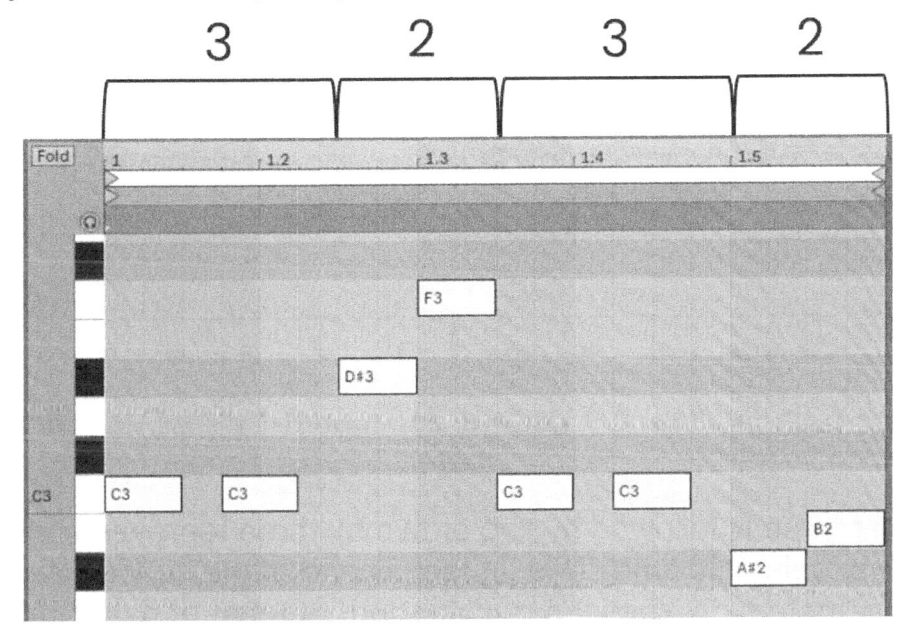

Figure 5.3: The Mission Impossible theme tune is in quintuple meter.

The ease with which this melody is heard and sung is because the five beats break down into simple groupings of three and two.

Another example of the use of this grouping—three beats followed by two beats—is *Down and Out* by Genesis. Its rhythm is shown in Figure 5.4:

Figure 5.4: Down and Out by Genesis, in quintuple meter, breaks down into a grouping of three followed by two.

In this track, the use of quintuple meter has an unsettling quality that suits the overall feel of the song

An example of a track in quintuple time that groups the beats the other way around (2+3) is Gorillaz' *5/4*. If you listen to the guitar strums with which the track begins, you will hear them being grouped into a set of two followed by a set of three, as shown in Figure 5.5. This strumming cycle is then repeated through much of the track.

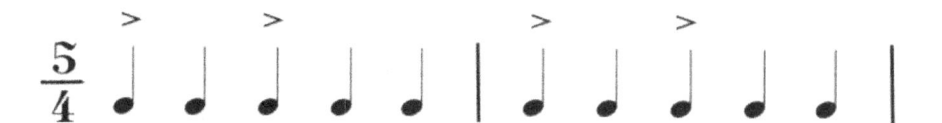

Figure 5.5: Gorillaz' 5/4 uses a 2+3 pattern within its quintuple meter.

Whether three is followed by two or two by three represents different *modes* of quintuple time. This, in fact, is one of the curious traits of irregular meters. Despite the nonstandard number of beats in the grouping, the emphases within the meter will tend to resolve into groupings of 2 or 3.

If you haven't tried using quintuple meter, give it a go. Simple quintuple meter has a count like this:

One, and, two, and, *three,* and, four, and five, and.

While compound quintuple meter has this kind of count:

One and and, two and and, three and and, *four* and and, five and and.

If you wish to write in quintuple time in your DAW, set its time signature to 5/4. If you want to use compound quintuple time, you can keep this time signature setting, but select a triplet grid for it. This will then give you fifteen sub-beats for each bar of the music.

Septuple Meter

Another possibility within the domain of irregular metric patterns is septuple meter, which comprises seven beats to the bar. Time signatures that may be used in simple septuple time are shown in Figure 5.6:

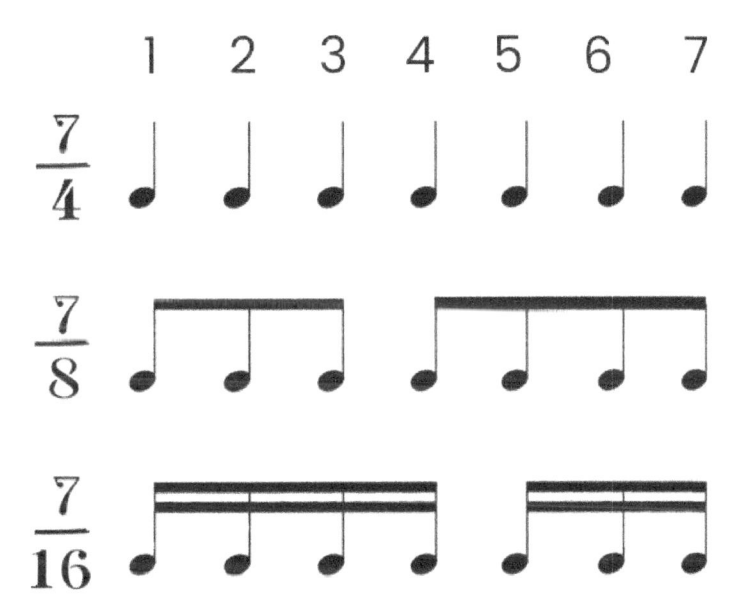

Figure 5.6: Septuple meter has 7 as its numerator.

Because there are seven beats to the bar in septuple meter, there are different ways in which these beats can be grouped. If you think of the number seven as being composed of 2 plus 2 plus 3, then there are three ways of ordering these groups, each counting as a distinct mode of septuple meter.

- 2+2+3
- 2+3+2
- 3+2+2

As you can see, there are three different groupings of emphasis available in septuple meter, and there is no reason that successive bars of septuple meter need to keep to the same grouping.

Septuple meter is a metric pattern that has a significant history of use, although admittedly, its use within classical music was rare, mostly confined to the more modern classical composers.

There is, however, an abundance of contemporary tracks that use septuple meter.

A notable example of the use of septuple meter is *Money* by Pink Floyd. When listening to this track, focus upon the bassline, as it is this which most readily reveals the seven beat pattern. Within the bassline, the seven beats are grouped into a 3-2-2 pattern, as shown in Figure 5.7:

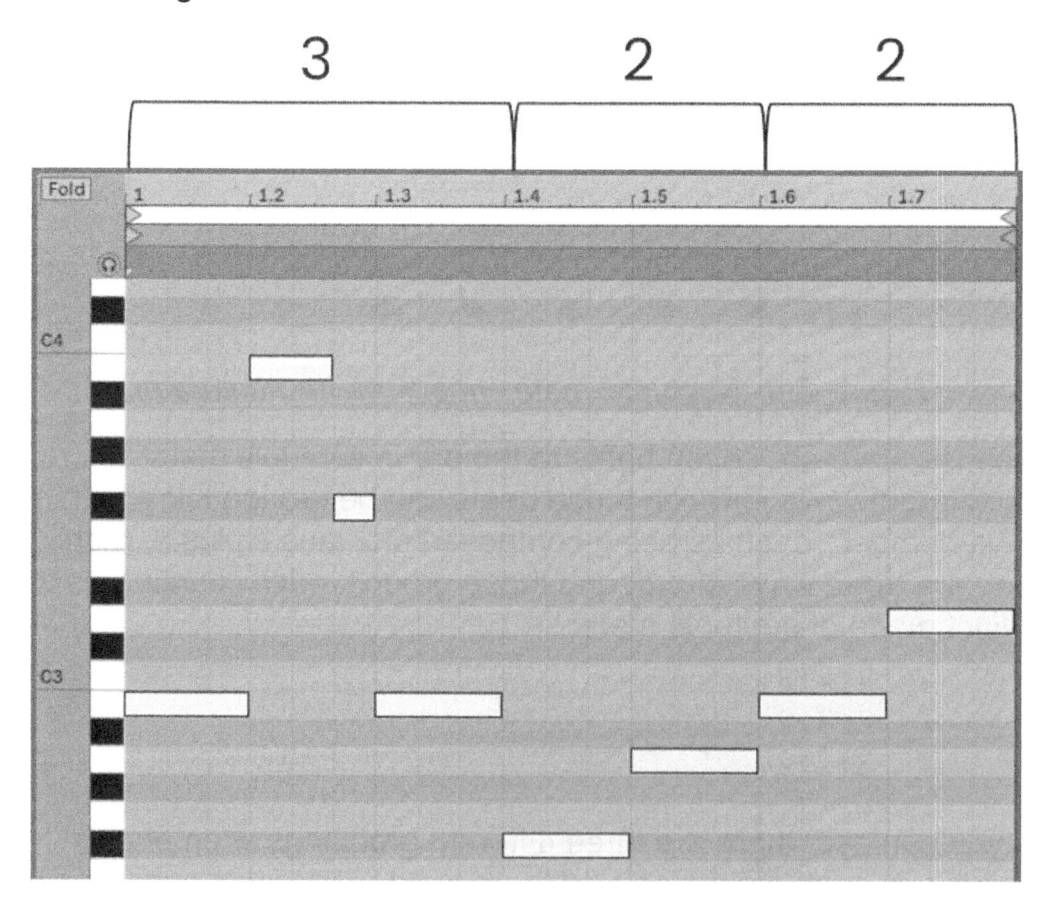

Figure 5.7: Money is written in compound septuple meter.

Also, we know it is written in compound septuple time because of the lone twelfth note in the middle of the first three beats, which fits neatly into the triplet grid.

A good track to listen to when studying septuple meter is the Wonder Woman theme by Hans Zimmer (titled *Themyscira*). This track is notable for its use of a rhythmic ostinato—a repeating rhythmic figure that runs through most of the track. The figure lasts for a single bar of the 7/8 time signature, as seen in Figure 5.8:

Figure 5.8: The ostinato in Zimmer's Themyscira.

In summary, septuple time is well worth experimenting with. Just remember to group your notes into a pattern of 3, 2 and 2 (in any order) to give your listener something to anchor themselves to.

Other Irregular Metric Patterns

Once you have got a handle on irregular meters, like quintuple and septuple time, other, more complex meters become much easier to understand. In the main, they result from the grouping of beats into twos and threes. So, for example, a meter that has a time signature of 11/8 can be understood as comprising three groups of three beats and one group of two beats.

3 +3+3+2

Alternatively, 11/8 could be approached as four groups of two beats and one group of three beats.

2ı2ı2ı2+3

These beat groups can be combined in any order, which creates several options, these being the different modes of 11/8. And when studying music that uses 11/8, the order of the groupings will always be a notable feature.

A good example of this is *Sagat's Theme From Streetfighter*, by Isao Abe, which divides the eleven beats into a group of six beats followed by a group of five beats, the former comprising two groups of three beats, the latter a group of two beats followed by a group of three beats.

One of the interesting features of this use of irregular meters is that, possibly because of their lack of symmetry, a certain mobility in using beat groups can be felt. Because of this, it is quite common for either the beat grouping or the meter itself to change throughout the track.

Obvious examples of this are *Here Comes the Sun* by George Harrison which juxtaposes 4/4 with 7/8 and 11/8. Another example is *Schism* by Tool which has bars in 5/8, 6/8 and 7/8. Yet another is *Say a Little Prayer* by Burt Bacharach which uses meters of 4/4, 10/4 and 11/4 through the song.

To understand this tendency to change meter in this fashion, it is a good policy to spend some time experimenting with the use of irregular meters. You will find that the irregular groupings have a knock-on effect upon how you think about the meter of your music. Rather than being a groove that the music then gets stuck in, the meter that you use develops a life of its own.

Exercises

1. Write a drum track in 7/4.
2. Write a melody in 11/8.
3. Write a drum track *and* a melody in 5/4.

CHAPTER 6: TOWARDS A VARIETY OF RHYTHMS

So far, we've looked at both regular and irregular meters. We have also seen that, whatever the meter, it will comprise a hierarchy of beats and sub beats that will characterise that meter. This hierarchy provides us with a platform for rhythmic invention.

There is, however, a significant benefit to pushing and stretching the boundaries of the metric pattern we are using using tried-and-tested techniques. In this chapter, we shall explore two such techniques: *syncopation* and *tuplets*.

Syncopation

As you know, a metric pattern comprises a hierarchy of beats and sub-beats that is then established in the listener's mind using stresses, i.e., the placing of accents upon primary beats in the bar. A good example of this is simple quadruple meter, in which the beats are grouped into pairs, showed by a stress on the first and third beats of the bar, as you can see in Figure 6.1:

Figure 6.1: In simple quadruple meter, stresses are placed on the first and third beats of each bar. The stress on the third beat is usually less than the stress on the first.

Syncopation is a rhythmic technique whereby the listener's expectation of this pattern of strong and weak beats is temporarily frustrated. This is achieved by placing the strong beat on what would normally be a weak beat of the bar. So, in the second bar of in Figure 6.2, the stresses have now been placed on the first and fourth beats, instead of the first and third:

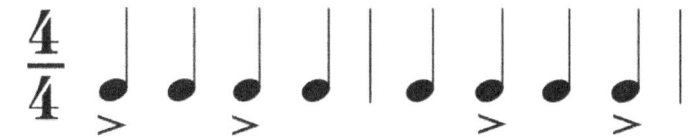

Figure 6.2: Syncopation subverts the listener's expectations of emphasis.

If you clap this rhythm, you will immediately discern the effect it has. It causes a release of energy caused by this temporary displacement of the strong beats.

The previous example could be extended further by substituting the second and third quarter notes of the bar for a half note. This then creates a motif that suggests syncopation. Try clapping the rhythm in Figure 6.3 and you will see what I mean:

Figure 6.3: Meter can also be subverted through the use of rests.

Unless you have some training in playing syncopated rhythms, you'll find it a challenge to play the second note of bar 2 with ease. This is because we are used to the stresses occurring on the ordinarily stronger parts of the bar.

Some great rhythmic effects can be achieved through use of syncopation, especially when the accentual displacement is perpetrated through several bars, like in Figure 6.4:

Figure 6.4: Syncopation extended across two bars.

This displacement could even be extended further, as shown in Figure 6.5:

Figure 6.5: Syncopation can be carried across many bars.

In Figure 6.5, from the second beat of bar 1, the 4/4 bar has essentially been pushed forward by a beat. This creates a great sense of energy to the rhythm, especially when, at the end of this cycle, the regular 4/4 bar is then re-engaged.

The implications of this use of syncopation are that shades of other metric patterns also emerge. We can appreciate this if we apply the scheme of accents belonging to the above example, but this time to a stream of quarter notes, as shown in Figure 6.6:

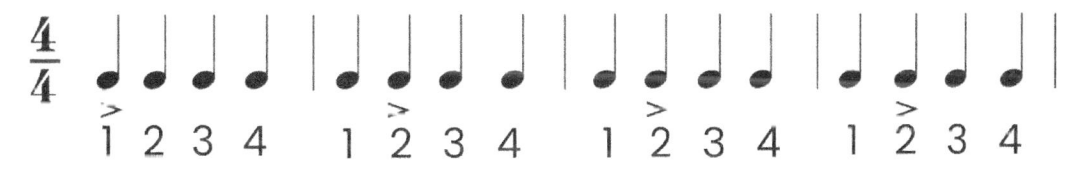

Figure 6.6: Implied groupings caused by syncopation.

We can see that accents are creating implied groupings of quarter notes, which in this case are a group of five, followed by two groups of four, followed by a group of three. In effect, therefore, we could get the same rhythmic effect if we wrote the above example like the example shown in Figure 6.7:

$$\frac{5}{4} \quad ♩ ♩ ♩ ♩ ♩ \quad | \frac{4}{4} \quad ♩ ♩ ♩ ♩ \quad | \quad ♩ ♩ ♩ ♩ \quad | \frac{3}{4} \quad ♩ ♩ ♩ |$$

Figure 6.7: The time signatures of the implied groupings caused by syncopation.

For modern music, syncopation is an important rhythmic device—one found in much of electronic music.

Tuplets and Triplets

Another technique that can stretch the boundaries of a metric pattern is the use of tuplets. Through use of tuplets, you will develop the ability to produce rhythms that have a subtle complexity to them.

Tuplets are the use of a group of beats or sub-beats that are, or seem to be, *borrowed* from a different meter. To explain this, let's consider the most basic tuplet of all, which is the duplet. The duplet is most used in compound meters. As you know, compound meter is where the beat breaks down into threes. A duplet is where a group of two beats are played in the same time as the usual three beats.

Figure 6.8 shows an example of duplets in the fourth beat of the bar. The meter is compound quadruple. Instead of having three sub-beats there, instead there are two. However, crucially, these two sub-beats are played in the same time as the usual three sub-beats, making it a duplet:

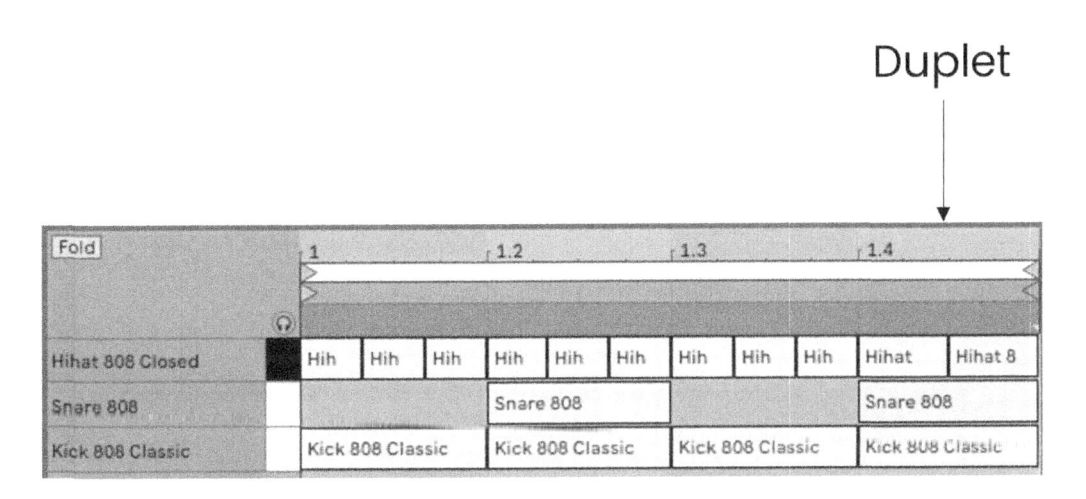

Figure 6.8: Duplets are two sub-beats where you'd expect three.

You can visualise duplets easily if we compare simple and compound triple time in Figure 6.9:

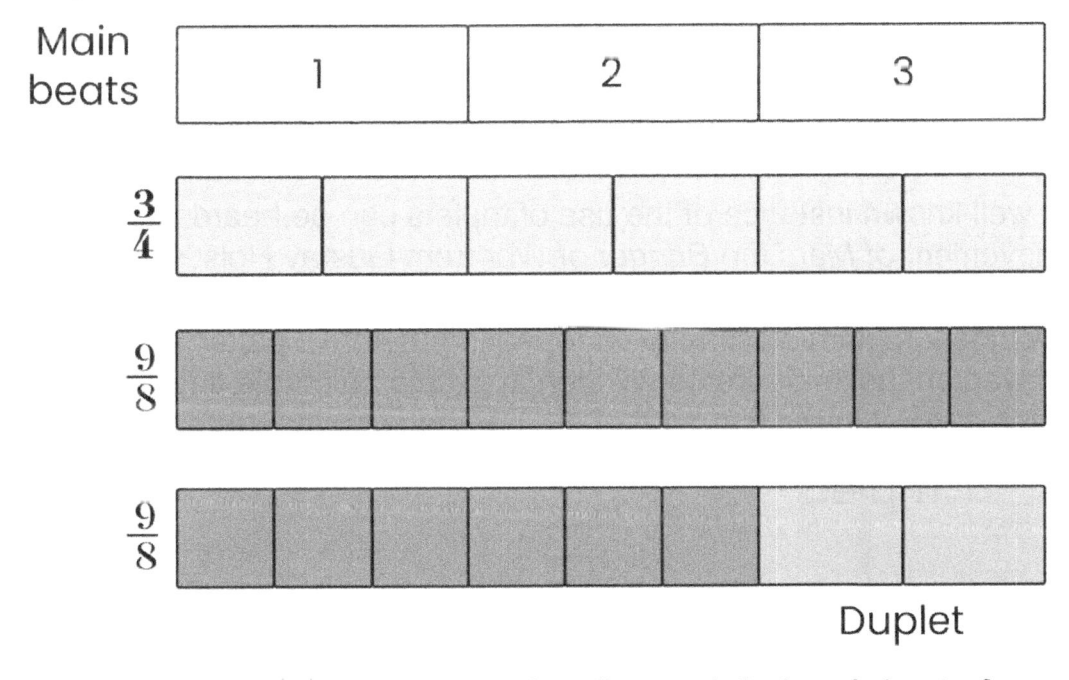

Figure 6.9: Duplets can be said to 'borrow' their sub beats from duple meter.

In simple meters, there is a similar phenomenon called triplets. In simple meter, the main beats of the bar break down into two sub-beats. A triplet uses three sub-beats in the same time of two, as in Figure 6.10:

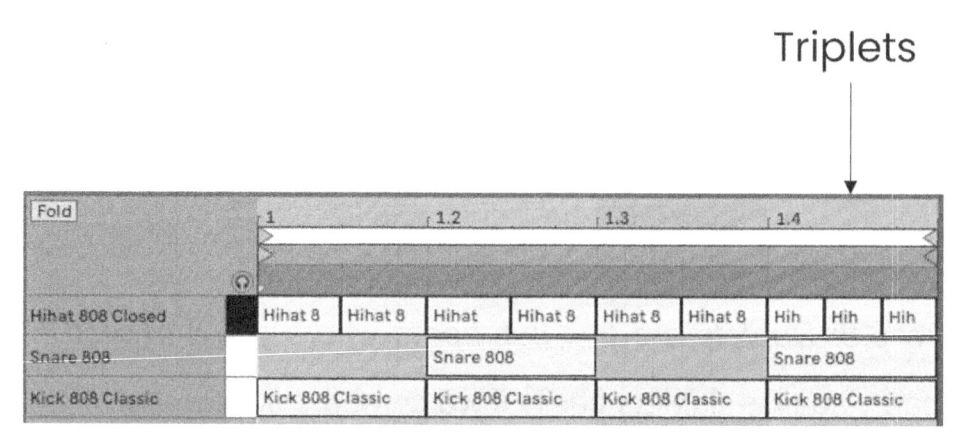

Figure 6.10: Triplets are three sub-beats where you'd expect two.

Notice that the fourth beat of the bar has three sub-beats instead of the expected two.

A well-known instance of the use of triplets can be heard in the movement *of Mars the Bringer of War* from Gustav Holst's *The Planet's Suite, Op. 32*. Running throughout most of this movement is a strident rhythmic ostinato—a repeating rhythmic pattern—that is played on the kettledrums. Written in simple quintuple time, Holst uses a triplet in the first beat of the bar, as seen in Figure 6.11:

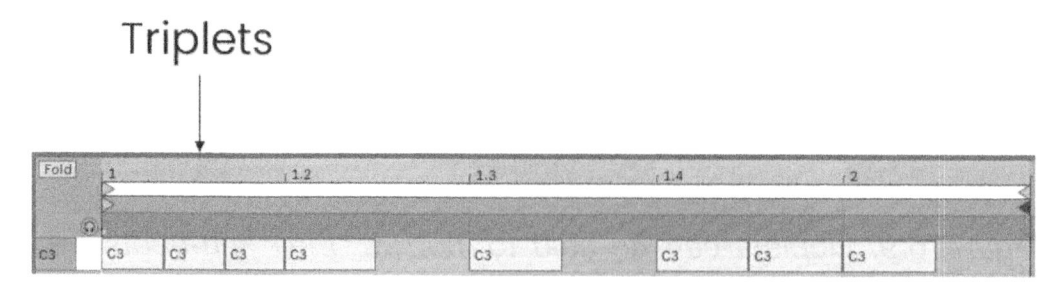

Figure 6.11: Triplets shown within Holst's Mars the Bringer of War.

This adds a sense of variety to what would otherwise be a straightforward rhythm in the simple quintuple meter.

More complex tuplets

Duplets (two where the prevailing meter calls for three), and triplets (three where the prevailing meter calls for two), are the most common form of tuplets. However, there are other forms of tuplets that are used less often, but still make musical sense. An example is in Figure 6.12—written in a standard 4/4 time signature, use is made of triplets, quintuplets and a pair of triplets:

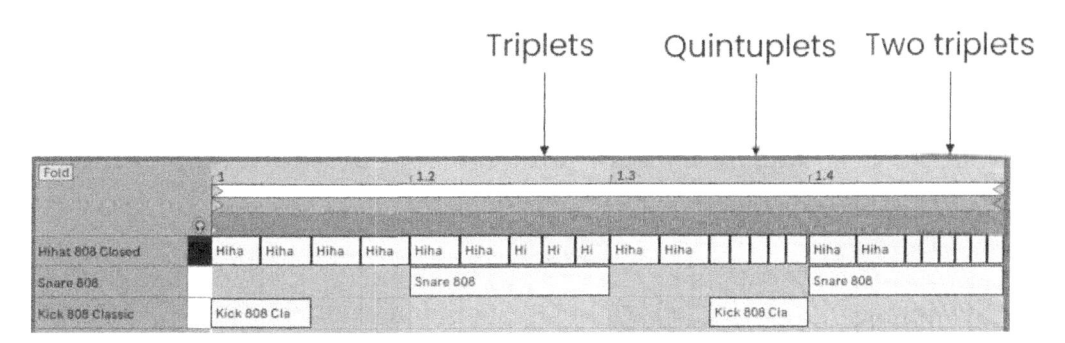

Figure 6.12: Triplets, quintuplets and a set of two triplets within a drum beat.

Key to these is a ratio comprising two numbers.

A ratio of:
- 2:3 signifies a group of two notes being played in the time of three—a duplet.
- 3:2 signifies a group of three notes being played in the time of two—a triplet.

- 4:3 signifies a group of four notes being played in the time of three—a quadruplet.
- 5:4 signifies five notes being played in the time of four—a quintuplet.
- 7:4 signifies seven notes being played in the time as four—a septuplet.

Used discretely, tuplets can create a significant effect—where the lead temporarily seems to uncouple from the surrounding elements. In this respect, tuplets that have higher numbers than the expected beat division (5:4, 7:4, etc.) create a speeding up effect, while tuplets that have lower numbers (2:3; 3:4; 7:8, etc.) create a gliding, slowing effect.

If you're working on a piece of music and you find the rhythm stale, consider using tuplets to create a more refined, interesting and complex rhythm.

Now that we have considered the use of tuplets, let's expand our knowledge of meter by exploring a new, and different way of thinking about it—*additive meter.*

Exercises

1. Write a simple 2-bar drum loop, with both bars identical.
2. Syncopate the second bar of this drum loop by changing the velocities of some drums and removing others.
3. Add a triplet and a quintuplet to the second bar of this drum loop.
4. Write a 4-bar melody, and experiment by adding three tuplets to it.

CHAPTER 7: ADDITIVE METER

The approach to meter that we studied in the earlier chapters of this book has a prevalent feature. It starts with the central concept of a bar, which is divided into beats, which is then broken down into a series of two (simple) or three (compound) sub-beats; each of which may be further broken down into a set of smaller time values. Notice that this represents a *divisive* approach to the building of metric patterns, because we divide the musical bar into smaller proportions. This is shown in Figure 7.1:

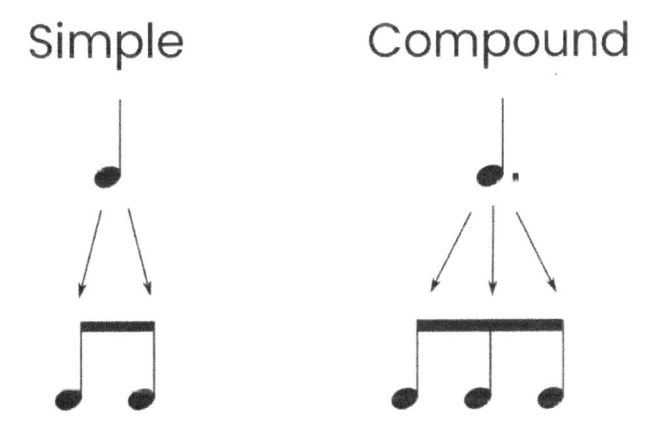

Figure 7.1: In divisive meter, beats are divided into smaller units.

DAW software is usually designed with a divisive approach in mind: new MIDI clips are often a bar long, which are then *divided* using the grid into smaller and smaller units of time.

The series of meters that logically result from this process comprise the classical system of meter. However, the divisive approach is not the only way of approaching meter, especially when considering the use of meter in a broader global context, that embraces both

Western and non-Western styles of music. Music is a global language, and the elements that modern music producers use are often drawn from musical traditions that span the globe.

Another approach to meter, one that is used in both modern Western and non-Western styles of music, is termed additive. The additive approach to meter takes a completely opposite tack to the divisive. Additive meter involves *adding* rhythmic units together, usually composed of groups of 2 and 3. This is done without trying to fit the meter into a specific time signature.

A well-known example of additive meter is the *Tresillo*, a rhythm used across Latin America, Africa and Asia. In the Tresillo, the fundamental meter is composed of 3+3+2, as seen in Figure 7.2:

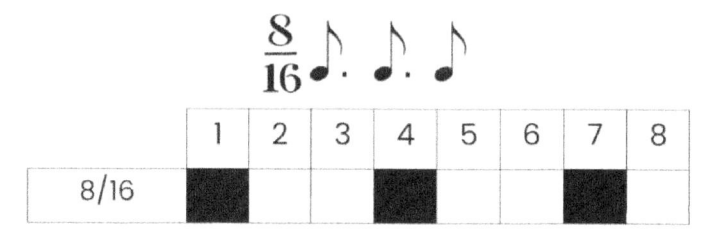

Figure 7.2: The tresillo expressed in notation and on a DAW grid.

As you can see, the bar (composed of eight sixteenth notes) does not divide equally in Tresillo, meaning that this meter is derived by *adding* the three time values together.

The difference between interpreting the Tresillo in a divisive manner and an additive manner is that in a divisive structure, the Tresillo *contrasts* with the beats of the meter, whereas in an additive structure, the Tresillo *is* the beats. If you want to read about this topic in greater depth, I particularly recommend the work of Victor Kofi Agawu. In the meantime, let's explore additive meter in more depth.

Another well-known example of additive meter in world music is called the *Clave*, which originated in sub-Saharan African music and is now found across many musical traditions, including Latin America and Louisiana. It is widely prevalent within the global African diaspora, with many variants of it used. The Clave is shown in Figure 7.3:

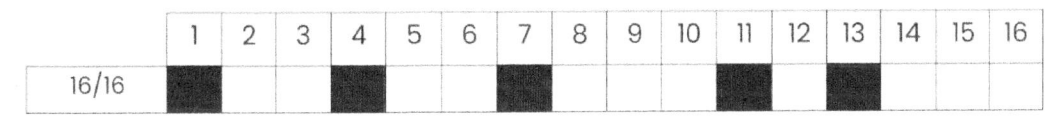

Figure 7.3: The Clave in a DAW's grid.

It is constructed from groupings of 2 or 3 notes, with a 2-note rest at 9 and 15.

Its time signature is sometimes written as 12/8, depending upon the meter of the other instrument parts, as seen in Figure 7.3:

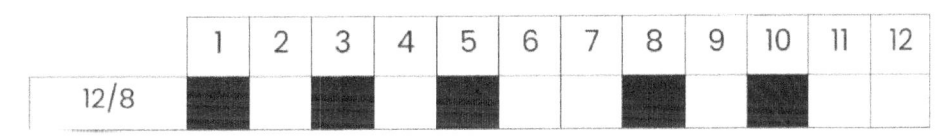

Figure 7.4: The Clave in a 12/8 time signature.

As you can see, additive meter lends itself to a distinct form of composition—one that is more dynamic and asymmetric than the structure of divisive meter.

A classic example of the use of additive meter is Mike Oldfield's *Tubular Bells*.

Written on paper, the time signature of this track changes a lot. This is because *Tubular Bells* is constructed using the principles of additive meter. Symptomatic of this is that the music comprises a cycle of three bars of 7/8 followed by a bar of 9/8.

This irregularity of meter is typical of an additive approach to metric construction. The rhythm is built from the ground up; the time signatures on paper are the time signatures that conform to the additive rhythm. We can see this if we examine the use of rhythmic cells, of which there are two types: duple, which is a group of two beats and triple, which is a group of three beats. Figure 7.5 shows the first bar:

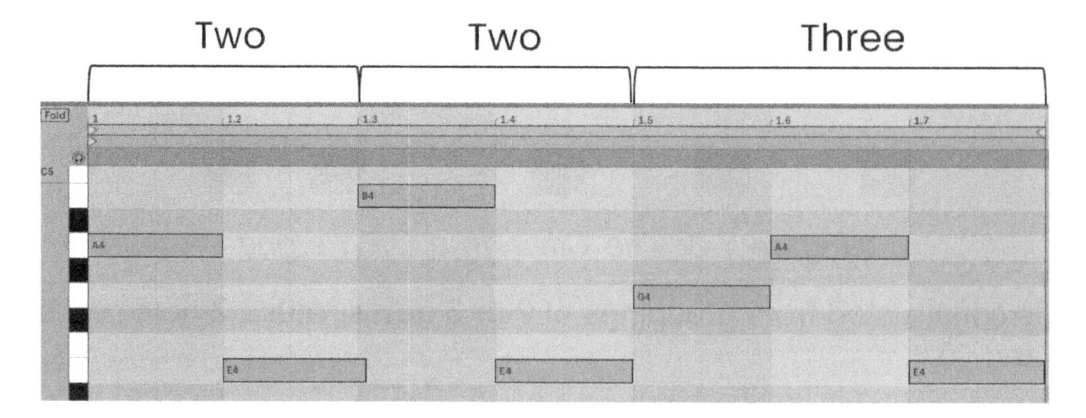

Figure 7.5: The first bar of Tubular Bells.

The second bar follows the same pattern in Figure 7.6:

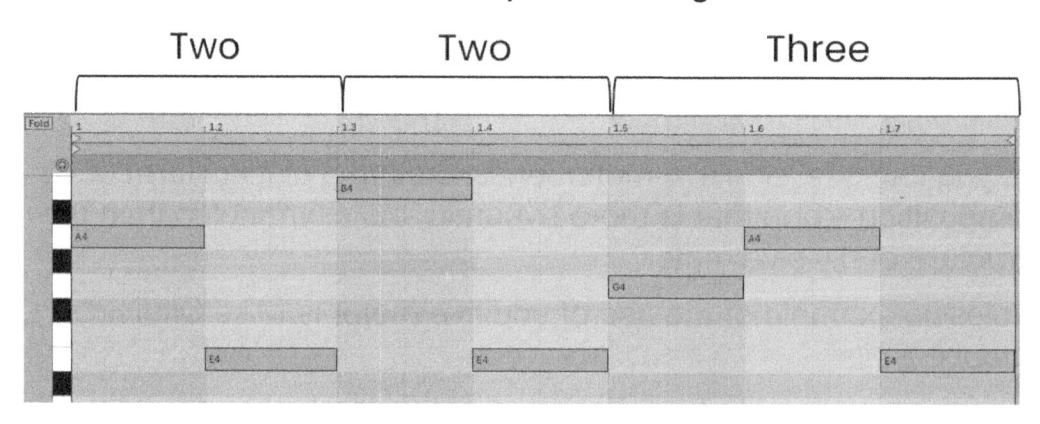

Figure 7.6: The second bar of Tubular Bells.

As does the third in Figure 7.7:

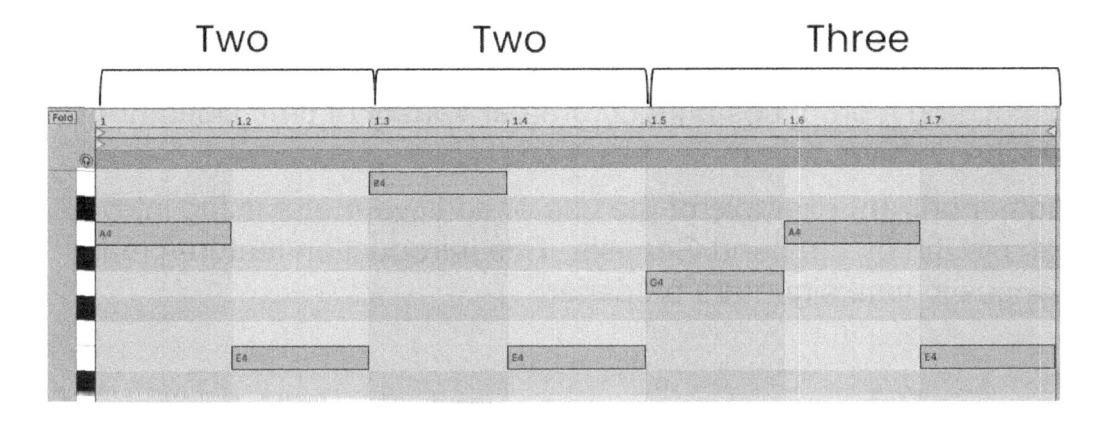

Figure 7.7: The third bar of Tubular Bells.

The fourth bar, however, provides a distinct pattern, as seen in Figure 7.8:

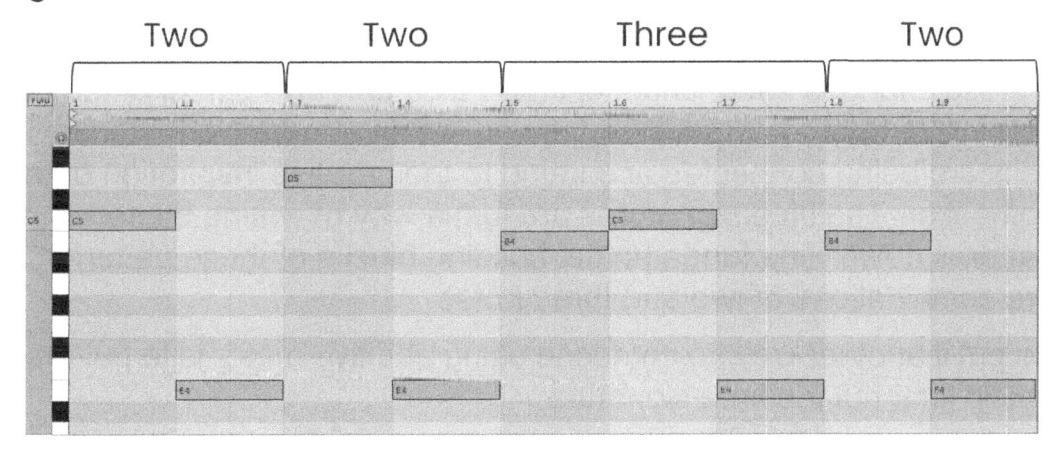

Figure 7.8: The fourth bar of Tubular Bells.

Put together, these four bars generate a pattern of numbers:
- 2+2+3
- 2+2+3
- 2+2+3
- 2+2+3+2

As you can see, Oldfield is building his meter from the ground up, using patterns of 2 and 3. This practice is the essence of additive rhythm, and it produces a much greater variety of time signatures than the divisive system.

Another brilliant example of the use of additive meter is the intro to Firth of Fifth by the band Genesis. This introduction features many changes in time signature on paper:

- 2/4
- 4/4
- 2/4
- 13/16
- 2/4
- 13/16 (four times)
- 15/16

If these changes seem chaotic, this is all a part and parcel of the use of additive rhythm. What is happening is that generative rhythmic cells are being connected according to the creative inspiration of the composer. The time signatures are just a way of writing these patterns down. The fundamental building blocks of these patterns are combinations of two and three notes.

To put it another way, to compose using additive meter is to put the music first, not the time signature.

Characteristic of additive meter is a sense of metric mobility, caused by adopting the sixteenth as the unit of addition. The result is a series of rhythms that not only have a great sense of continuity—caused by continual references to the rhythmic unit—but also a great sense of variety, caused by the shifting of the downbeat at the start of the rhythmic cells.

For another example of the use of additive rhythm, let's look at the first two bars of *Etude No. 2* by Philip Glass. A prolific user of additive meters, for this piece, Glass takes the eighth note to be his rhythmic unit. The first bar has a time signature of 7/8, comprising a grouping of eighth notes into a four (2+2) and a three. The second bar has a time signature of 4/4, and comprises a grouping of eighth notes into two groups of four (2+2), as shown in Figure 7.9:

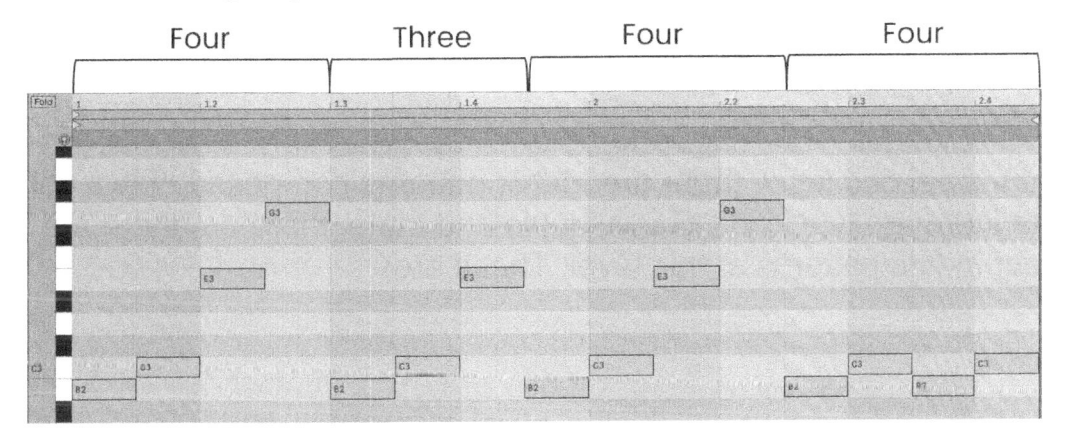

Figure 7.9: The first two bars of Etude No. 2 by Philip Glass.

Glass then uses this scheme of paired bars through the rest of the piece.

With that in mind, let's explore how to create an additive meter.

The first step is to select a single, short, unit of time — the rhythmic unit. This unit can be whatever note value that you choose for it: quarter notes, eighth notes, sixteenth notes. This represents the unit of time that will then be subjected to additive procedures.

Looking at the matter logically, it becomes apparent that additive meter can only comprise groups of 2 or 3 units. This is because any larger number will itself comprise groups of 2 or 3.

At core, therefore, additive meter is simple. We're simply experimenting with groups of 2 and 3 beats. Called generative cells, these groups can be combined in any order or number. They can also be maintained as a fixed pattern, or they can be changed. This is one of the significant features of additive meter: it is infinitely flexible and offers the user an infinite variety of metric patterns.

So, let us look at the metric patterns that become available to us. For convenience, we will take a sixteenth to be our rhythmic unit. At the first level, there are metric patterns composed of just one cell. As there are two kinds of cells, these are:

- 2/16
- 3/16

At the second level, there are metric patterns composed of two cells. As there are two kinds of cell, duple and triple, therefore there are four metric patterns at this level. These are:

- 2+2—2/8
- 2+3—5/16
- 3+2—5/16
- 3+3—6/16

At the third level, there are metric patterns composed of three cells. As there are two kinds of cells, there are therefore eight metric patterns at this level. These are:

- 2+2+2—3/8
- 2+2+3—7/16
- 2+3+2—7/16
- 3+2+2—7/16
- 2+3+3—8/16
- 3+2+3—8/16
- 3+3+2—8/16 (this is the *Tresillo* meter discussed earlier in the chapter)
- 3+3+3—9/16

As the number of groupings increase, a pattern emerges, as shown in Table 7.1:

Table 7.1: The number of time signatures and note grouping combinations depends on the number of groupings used.

Number of groupings	Number of time signatures	Number of possible combinations
0	0	0
1	2	2
2	3	4
3	4	8
4	5	16
5	6	32
6	7	64

As you can see, as the number of groupings range increases, the number of combinations increases exponentially.

Use of additive meter

As you have already seen, an additive meter is built from a small note value up.

The great thing about additive meter is that you have an incredible flexibility in terms of the range of meters that you would like to use. With this in view, I would thoroughly recommend that you spend some time learning to use additive meters practically. For this purpose, use a hand drum if possible; if you don't have one then even the side of a desk will work. The important part of the exercise is learning to play rhythms within an additive metric framework.

Through playing additive rhythms, you discover that stress is how you generate the individual cells of 2 or 3. The first in the cell requires emphasis—be it the use of a root note, a different drum tone, or simply more volume. We'll look at these techniques in more detail later in the chapter.

As you experiment with different additive patterns, you may find that they each possess their own character and feeling. It is down to you, as the musician, to decide what that character and feeling is. This is just like the feel that you might ascribe to a particular mode, i.e. major or minor.

Something that will help your progress through the world of additive meter is starting off with the simplest metric patterns. If you like, start off with a single generative cell. Then go on to two cells, whether of 2 or 3. Then you'll have four patterns to experiment with: 2+2, 2+3, 3+2 and 3+3. Then, when you feel ready, go on to those patterns that involve three groups of 2 or 3. In this way, you can work your way methodically through the various metric patterns that the world of additive meter offers.

Once you've done this, it is useful to bring a melodic element into play. Select a group of three notes, say, for example, A, D and E. Assign A to the strong beat of a group of two or three. Assign D to the second beat of a group of two or three. Finally, assign E to the third beat of a group of three. Although this is a rather mechanical approach, it will help you appreciate the value of additive meter at a melodic, as well as rhythmic level.

Let's explore the use of additive meter within DAW software.

Use of additive meters using DAW software

There are certain techniques that can make it easier to use additive meter within a DAW.

You can, of course, program in a time signature that would suit the step cycle that you're using. A good example of this would be a seven-step cycle composed of 3+2+2. Now, you could set your time signature to 7/16, which would establish a sixteenth note as your rhythmic unit. Should at any point you then want to change the meter, you can, of course, program that change in at the requisite point in the track. However, this may be unsuitable should you wish to have different additive loops of different meters within your work.

Another approach to the use of additive meter within your DAW is to think of your step cycles as being loops of a certain length. Those who are used to using step sequencers will understand how easy this can be. A step sequencer allows you to pre-program a specified sequence of notes/rests, triggered either by running the step sequencer or by playing and holding MIDI notes.

For example, in Figure 7.10, Reason's Matrix pattern sequencer has a pattern of 3+3+3 programmed in. The step cycle length of 9 and the resolution of 1/16 means that the pattern loops in nine 16th notes.

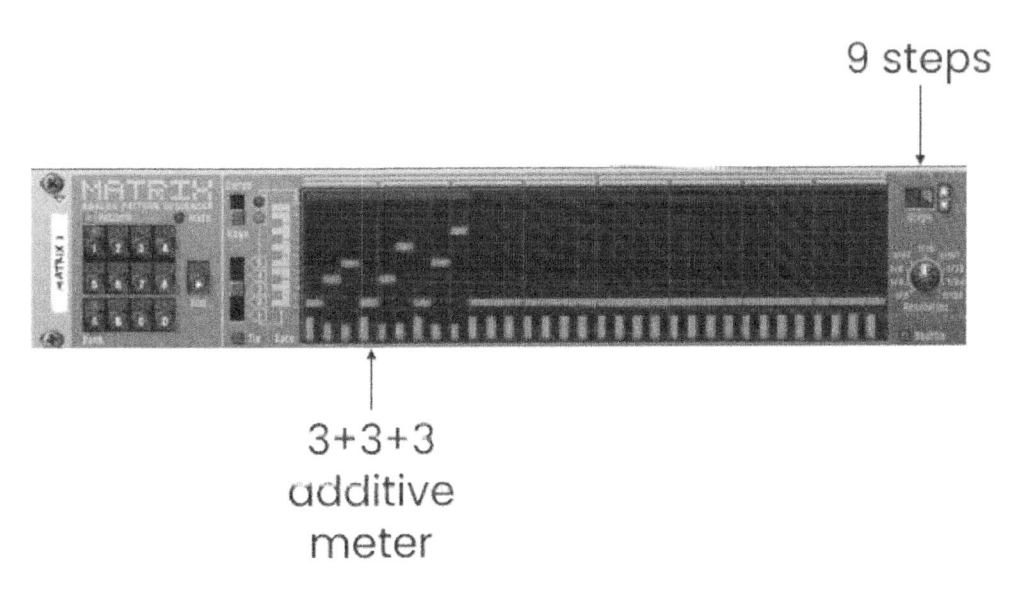

Figure 7.10: Additive meter created in a step sequencer.

However, step sequencers have a limited use. If you have many of them in a track, it's burdensome to write in the automation data to trigger them at the right time.

Alternatively, you can use the loop function of your DAW. To do this, simply write in your pattern, then trim the size of the loop to the size of your step cycle.

For example, consider a 3+2+3+3 meter composed of eleven 16th notes. This meter can be looped by changing the loop length to eleven 16th notes. Doing so means that the meter will always loop to a duration of eleven sixteenths, as seen in Figure 7.11 using Ableton Live:

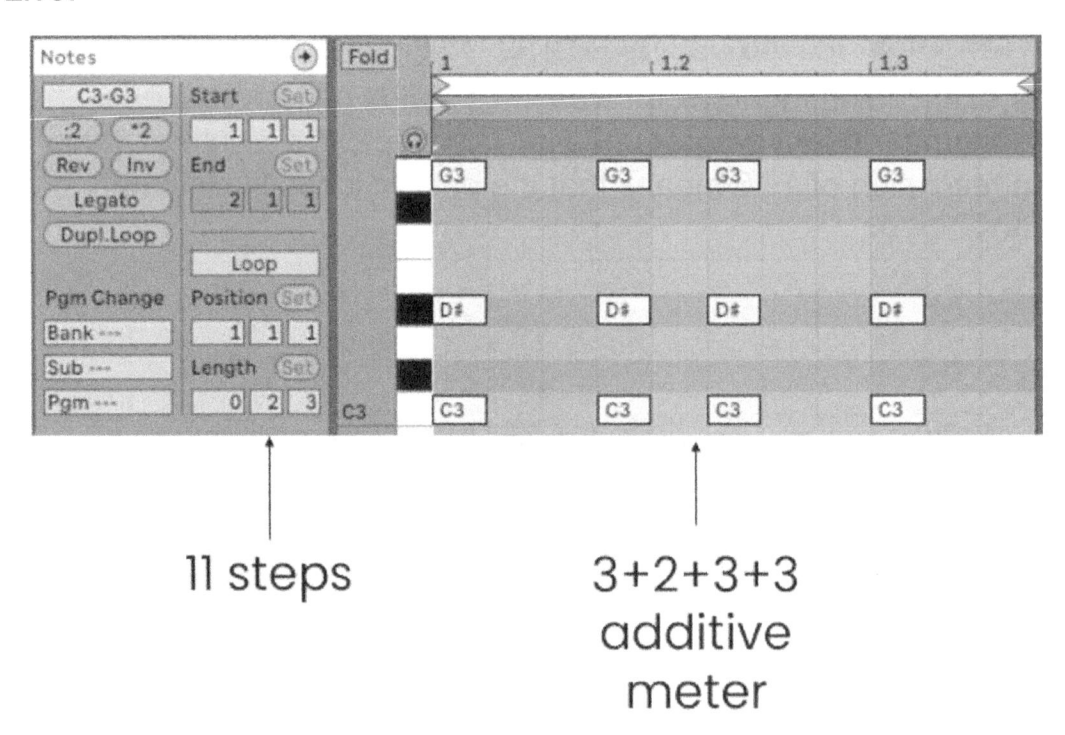

Figure 7.11: Additive meter created in a DAW's grid.

This approach is especially helpful when you seek to sequence your track. If you drag this clip into Arrangement view, loop it by dragging the right-hand side of the clip to the right. This means that even though the time signature of the project is 4/4, the clip remains a loop of eleven sixteenths—as you can see in Figure 7.12.

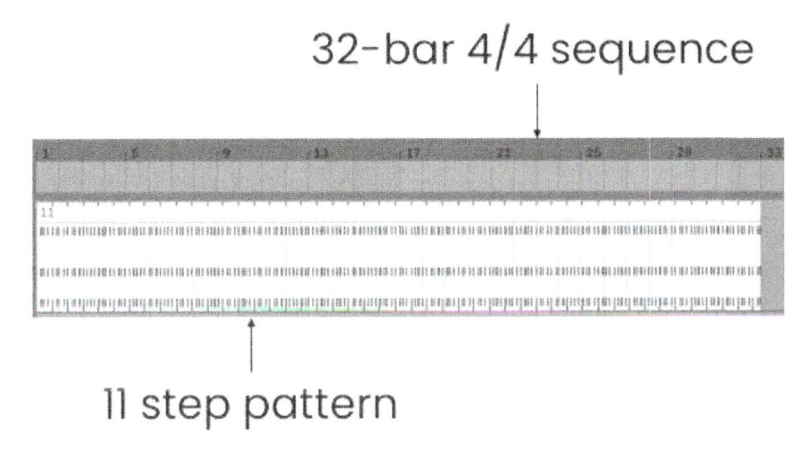

Figure 7.12: Additive meter looped over 32 bars of 4/4.

Stress programming

We've already considered how metric patterns imply a natural hierarchy of beats, in which some beats receive more stress than others. This is because of the need to emphasise certain beats according to their status as a part of the metric pattern.

The first beat of each cycle is clearly the most important and would therefore receive the strongest stress. If not, your listener is going to find it difficult to perceive the step cycles you might be using. After the first beat of the bar, the first beat of each subsequent cell will receive a stress, so that your listener will perceive the pattern of cells that you have used.

The best way to do this is to imagine yourself playing a step cycle on a drum, or perhaps using a piano. Naturally, you will put an emphasis on the correct beats of the step cycle as you are playing.

However, playing a step cycle is one thing, while programming it into a DAW is another. Clearly, what we want is a scheme applied to particular beats of the step cycle that would reflect how a musician might naturally play.

There are several ways to do this, but the easiest is to program the velocities into your MIDI clip, as shown in Figure 7.13:

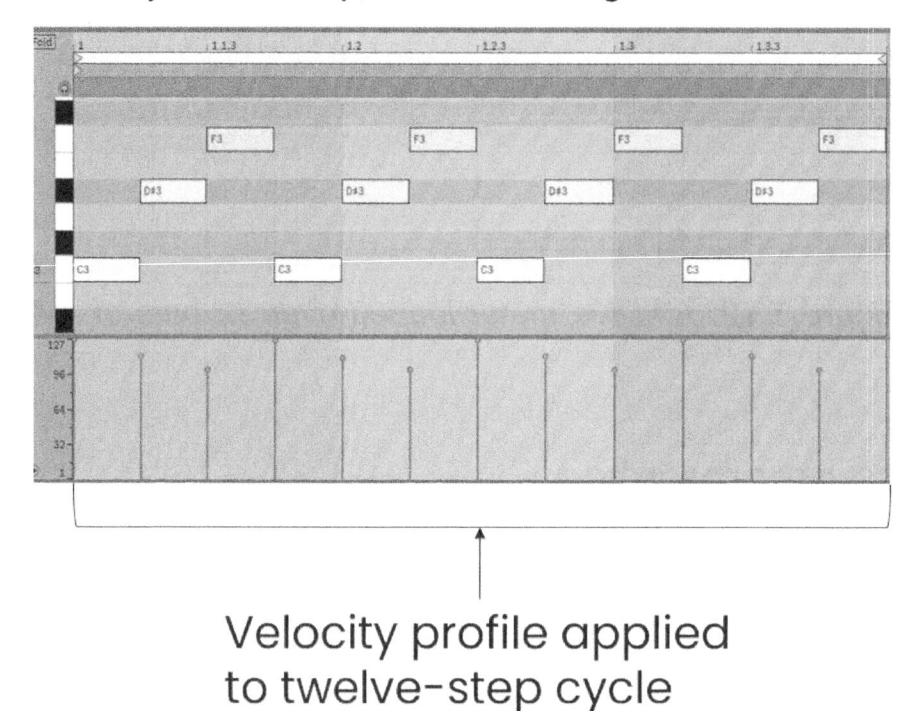

Velocity profile applied to twelve-step cycle

Figure 7.13: Velocity used to create emphasis.

As you can see, the first note of each rhythmic cell has a higher velocity than the remaining notes.

For many virtual instruments, this may be enough to add emphasis to the first note of each cell. However, for some virtual synthesizers, you may need to do more. Here, you will need to route the MIDI velocity to either the filter cutoff or the volume to add this emphasis, just like I have done in Sylenth1 in Figure 7.14:

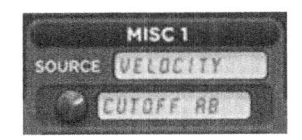

Figure 7.14: Velocity routed to filter cutoff.

When programming stresses into additive cycles, be sensitive to both the context and nuance that a cycle might gain. So, for example, if you have a melodic loop comprising a series of arpeggios, the base notes of the arpeggio will probably stand out for themselves—in which case you can be a lot more subtle with how you program the stresses of your step cycle. In these situations, let your ear be the ultimate guide—when you're auditioning your track, you will soon pick up on the features that a melodic or rhythmic pattern operating within the bounds of a step cycle will need.

Additive meter, once you understand it, can be a great a framework for your rhythmic invention.

For example, if you find yourself stuck in a divisive 4/4 rut, look at the sixteen-step cycle from an additive metrical viewpoint—what interesting combinations of additive cells can you use to generate more interesting rhythms?

As soon as you experiment with additive meter, you will no doubt recognise it when you hear it in other people's tracks. This is because many music producers have already developed a sense of additive rhythm, and are embracing the possibilities that it offers.

Now that we've built a great foundation in using meter, let's explore a more challenging concept: polymeter.

Exercises

1. Create an additive loop composed of seven 1/16th notes, using cells of 3+2+2.

2. Create two copies of this loop.
3. Use velocity and/or note choices to change the articulation of the copies—change one to 2+3+2, and the other to 2+2+3.
4. Compare the differences between each loop.

CHAPTER 8: POLYMETER

Polymeter is the use of two or more meters *at the same time*. The rhythmic unit of each meter remains the same, but the number of units is different.

As an example, picture a loop of 4 beats, playing over a loop of 3 beats, as shown in Figure 8.1:

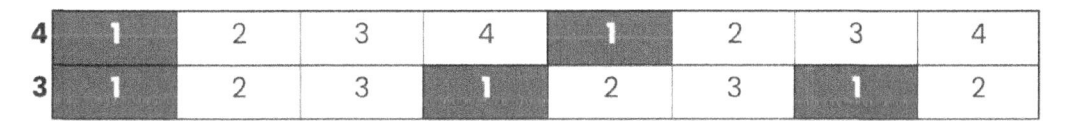

4	**1**	2	3	4	**1**	2	3	4
3	**1**	2	3	**1**	2	3	**1**	2

Figure 8.1: A loop of 4 beats playing over a loop of 3 beats. Notice that the emphasis of the first beat diverges.

The '1' at the start of each loop is emphasised, meaning that the two downbeats (i.e. the beats with emphasis) are not always synchronised in each bar. This gives the listener the feeling that the two loops move in and out of sync with each other over time, creating a dynamic, shifting feeling. This is the fundamental idea behind polymeter.

The history behind the use of polymeter

Polymeter is a timeless rhythmic technique, present in musical styles around the world for centuries.

A prominent example of modern classical polymeter use is Steve Reich's *Drumming*, where the moving downbeats create a hypnotic, restless rhythm.

Examples of polymeter in contemporary music include:

- *Touch and Go* by the Cars uses 5/4 time for the drums but 4/4 time for the other layers.
- *Kashmir* by Led Zeppelin is now a famous example of the use of polymeter, in which 4/4 time is used in one part and 3/4 in another.
- *Pink Mist* by Gunship has drums in 4/4 time while other layers make use of 7/8.
- *Frame by Frame* by King Crimson features two guitar parts—one of which is in 7/8 meter while the other is in 13/16.
- *5/4* by Gorillaz has the drums in a 4/2 time signature creating a great polymetric effect.
- *Secret Liaison* by Source Direct is a classic example of a prominent technique in jungle music, where the downbeat of the break sample constantly shifts to create a great deal of rhythmic complexity.

Using polymeter in your music

For many of you reading this, your music will primarily be loop-based. You may even use DAW software that is designed around the use of loops, such as Ableton or Bitwig. Polymeter is therefore a vital tool to use in your compositions.

Used correctly, polymeter can:

1. Create layers of sub-meter sitting over your prevalent meter, adding a new rhythmic dimension to your work.
2. Bring percussion to life.
3. Give your music a sense of 'funk' that it has previously lacked.

In polymeter, one or more layers of music are deliberately de-synchronised from the prevailing meter. This is done by assigning to them their own metric cycle that plays simultaneously with the prevailing metric cycle. Now, as the rhythmic unit is preserved, means that at certain points, these polymetric layers will fall in and out of sync with one another. The points at which they do this, will of course, all depend upon the meters being used. If a step cycle of, say, seven sixteenths is being used in one layer and the prevailing meter is 4/4, the layers will fall back into sync once every seven bars.

Let's explore polymeter in more depth with some practical examples. You can listen to all these examples at https://meter.producers.guide.

Example One: 8:5

A great place to start with polymeter is by using it to improve a drum beat. A 2/4 drum beat (i.e., in simple duple meter), such as one used in minimal Techno, can become tiresome. Great melodic elements sometimes aren't enough to bring the listener's interest back.

This is where polymeter comes in.

A 5/16 pattern juxtaposed with a 2/4 drum beat creates a fascinating rhythm, with the 5/16 pattern slowly synchronising and desynchronising with the pattern of the kick and the snare.

Figure 8.2 is an example:

	1	2	3	4	5	6	7	8
Kick	■				■			
Hi-hat			■				■	
Clap					■			
Rimshot	■	■		■				

Figure 8.2: An 8/16 cycle playing over a 5/16 cycle.

As you can see, there are two different loop lengths: the top three loops comprise eight sixteenths, and the bottom loop comprises five sixteenths. When looped together, they create a macro pattern that runs for forty quarter notes before it repeats, since 5 × 8 = 40.

In the listener's mind, this breaks the loop out of the dull framework of a single, repeating bar, creating a narrative that draws the listener in. Thanks to the addition of a single polymeter, the drum beat has been transformed from a loop comprising one bar of 2/4 to one that maintains the listener's interest for much longer.

Example Two: 16:3

This is one of the most prominent, regularly used polymetric techniques in electronic music—and for good reason.

16:3 comes from a 4/4 prevailing meter (for example a 4/4 drum beat), combined with a loop lasting three 16th notes. This creates a loop whereby the downbeat of the 3/16 meter contrasts neatly with the beats of the 4/4.

In the example in Figure 8.3 below, I've combined a 2/4 sine bleep riff with a 4/4 drum track and an acid bassline lasting three sixteenths.

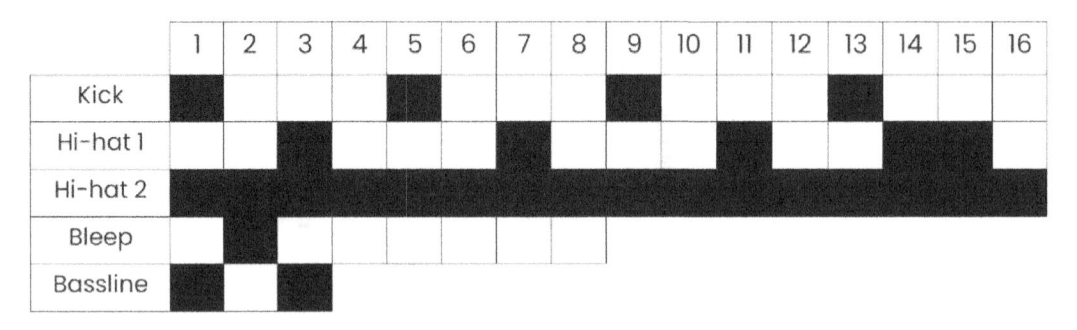

Figure 8.3: A 4/4 pattern playing with a 3/16 pattern.

This has created an interesting interaction between the drums, bleep, and bassline. The polymetric bassline makes for a repetition point every three bars. The bleep sounds like it *should* be polymetric given its location in the loop, but it in fact grounds the listener, making the bassline seem more rhythmically contrasting.

If you listen carefully, you'll start hearing polymetric 3/16 motifs *everywhere* in electronic music. They're simple, elegant, and create a ceaseless energy.

Listen out for them in these contexts:

- Electronic 'bleeps' designed to create an extra layer of energy without detracting too much from the underlying layers. An example is 4:02 onwards in George Fitzgerald's *Lights Out*.
- Sub-bass lines in bass music, where the contrast between the 4/4 drum beat and the 3/16 bass sounds *massive* on a big sound system. An example is *Paper House* by Skeptical and DRS.
- A 3/16 delay used to create faded repetitions of a note or chord stab (yes, this counts as polymeter!). An example is *Anchor* by Forest Drive West.

Example Three: 9:7:4:3

A more complex example is to 'stack' more than one polymeter together to create something more dynamic.

An example could be:

1. A 4/4 kick creating a prevailing meter of 4/4
2. A 3/16 sub-bass
3. A 9/16 sequence of chord stabs
4. A 7/16 chord stab

The result is a complex polymetric texture, as shown in Figure 8.4:

	1	2	3	4	5	6	7	8	9
A7min chord	A		A			A		A	
Amin/E chord	A								
4/4 kick	K								
Bass	A3	E3	E3						

Figure 8.4: A combination of nine, seven, four and three-16th cycles.

As you can see, the two chords sit on a 7/16 and a 9/16 cycle, respectively. This means that their repeating point is sixty-three beats. However, the 3/16 bass means the reporting point is almost 48 bars—a great opportunity for some truncation, as I'll explain later in this chapter.

Played alongside the 7/16 and 9/16 loops, the 3/16 bass and 4/4 kick anchor the whole arrangement.

The result is a piece of Techno that is rhythmically more complex than most tracks that are currently released. This is despite the sheer simplicity of the underlying mathematical principles.

A shown, there's absolutely no reason not to push the boundaries with a more adventurous polymetric approach. It's easy to do, and in my opinion, too few producers explore it in any great depth.

In the following section, I'll show you techniques to help you use polymeter in your own work.

Session View

Whereas to work in a polymetric fashion using non-electronic instruments (such as guitars and drums) may take years of practice, it's easy to do with electronic music.

Clips within Session View in Ableton are the easiest way to work in a polymetric fashion (just as they are with additive meter). These are shown in Figure 8.5. You can set the clip lengths to whatever you want, and they will automatically loop when they reach the end, allowing you to hear your polymeter in full.

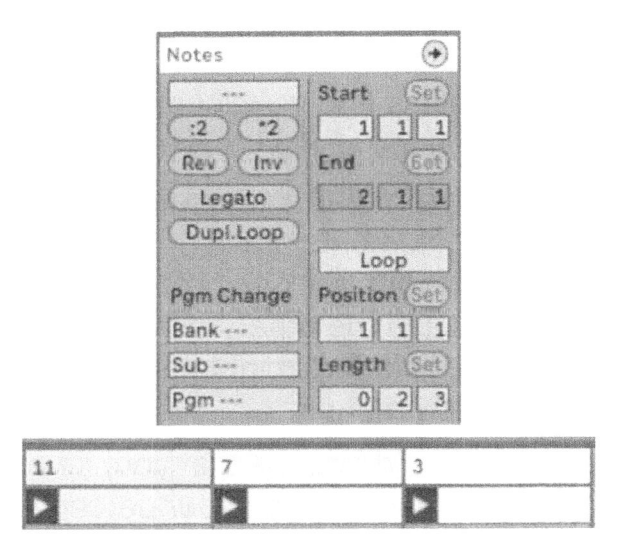

Figure 8.5: Top: A clip in Ableton set to a loop length of 11/16. Bottom: Three loops playing in Ableton's Session View, creating a polymeter.

Logic Pro X has implemented a similar feature called *Live Loops*, and Bitwig Studio has a very similar feature.

In the long-term, I would expect that all DAWs will adopt this approach, but if your DAW doesn't have an Ableton-like clip launcher, you can still easily create polymeters. Consider, for example:

- Using multiple step sequencers;
- Adding loops to your sequencer over a very long period of time, e.g. 128 bars;

- Sampling your own work to use in creative sampling software.

Anchoring

Anchoring is an important concept to consider when working in polymeter. In polymeter, we're stretching the listener's perception of the prevailing meter by juxtaposing it with a contrasting meter.

Most of your listeners, unless they're exceptionally skilled musicians, will only be able to hear your music in one meter.

When working with a single meter, this wouldn't even be a consideration—if all your elements are in 4/4, there's no question that your listener will hear your track as being in 4/4. However, if half your elements are in 4/4, and the other half are in 3/4, there's a chance that some of your listeners might hear your track in 3/4 or feel pulled between the two meters.

What makes this even more difficult is that you, as a producer, may not even be able to hear this effect, as *your* perception of your work is anchored in 4/4.

The solution to this is to ensure that your listener is anchored to the meter that you want them to be anchored to. There are several ways in which you can accomplish this, once you've decided on the meter that you want your listener to be anchored to:

1. Set the first eight bars of your track to the meter that you want your listener to be anchored to, and only add the polymetric elements later. This means that your listener is likely to hear the prevailing, anchoring meter throughout the track.
2. Ensure that the heavier, more dominant parts of your mix sit within the anchoring meter, for example, the kickdrum and the snare.
3. If you want one of your more dominant elements to deviate from your anchoring meter, make sure at least

two other dominant elements sit within your anchoring meter. For example, if your lead vocal is in a different meter to your anchoring meter, try to keep your kick and your bass in the anchoring meter. If your bass is in a different meter, keep your kick and melodic lead within your anchoring meter.

A good test of whether your work is sufficiently anchored in your chosen meter is to count out loud over your music—first, count in the time of your anchoring meter. Then, count in the time of one of your alternate meters. If your perception of the track's meter changes drastically when you undertake this second count, it's likely that your listeners will have the same issues listening to your work.

You could, of course, choose to cut your listener loose—with the correct balance of elements, you can create an audial illusion, where some of your listeners hear your work in one meter, and others hear it in another! Just make sure you're not doing so accidentally.

Truncate your polymeters

Even though polymeters are highly prevalent in electronic music, it's rare for a polymetric loop to play throughout a track without an additional element bringing the loop back in line with the prevailing meter. I call this element a truncation.

When there is a complex polymeter playing (for example, 3/16+5/16+7/16 in a 4/4 track), this can sometimes bewilder—the listener can feel adrift. Truncation is a helpful way of keeping the listener correctly anchored, as well as bringing a sense of funk into your polyrhythm. Here are some examples of truncation, beginning with Figure 8.6:

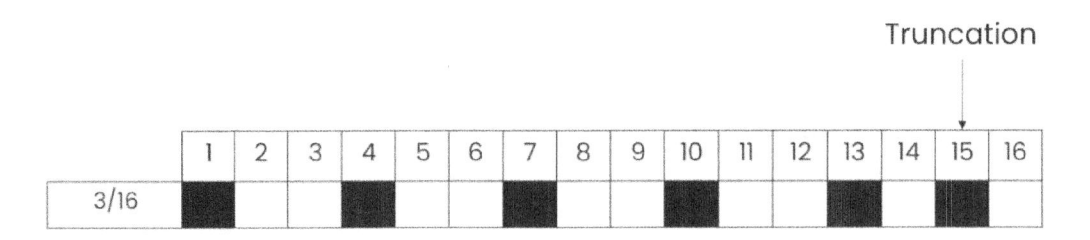

Figure 8.6: A truncated 3/16 pattern.

In this example, the 3/16 polymeter should appear at grid number 16, then continue from 3 in the next bar. However, it has been truncated, in that the last note is in line with the original 4/4 rhythm. You may notice that this, in isolation, creates the *Clave* additive meter.

Truncation can also occur at the start of a bar, for example in the 32-step sequence shown in Figure 8.7. The 5/16 polymeter should continue at step 4 after the first 32 steps, but it, in fact, reverts to the first step:

Figure 8.7: Truncation occurring at the start of a five-step pattern over thirty-two steps.

You can experiment a great deal with this effect when working with polymeter. Try anchoring the listener every bar, every two bars, even every sixty-four bars. Broadly, shorter truncation periods (such as one or two bars) give the listener a brief sense of polymeter within a stable overall rhythm. Longer truncation periods (such as thirty-two or sixty-four bars) give the listener a long time immersed in the polymeter, at a risk of a sense of rhythmic instability.

You'll find each track has its own correct point at which to truncate, if at all!

To conclude, polymeter is a simple, yet highly effective method of vastly increasing the rhythmic complexity of your music. I recommend you try it with the exercises at the end of this chapter.

In the long-term, I recommend you experiment iteratively in many polymeter, combining different prevailing meters with polymetric layers of various lengths. You may discover a rarely used but highly effective combination of meters.

In the next chapter, we shall take our knowledge a step further by exploring the art of polyrhythm.

Exercises

1. Create a 4/4 drum track.
2. Add a melodic additive loop that is 7 sixteenth notes in length.
3. Add a bassline that is 3 sixteenth notes in length.

CHAPTER 9: POLYRHYTHM

In the previous chapter, we discussed the use of polymeter—the art of combining multiple meters, creating variable bar lengths for each meter. Polyrhythm is also the art of combining more than one meter. With polyrhythm, however, the *overall bar length is the same for all meters*.

The process of polyrhythm produces rhythmic units of different relative lengths. A good example of this is the use of 4/4 in one part and 3/4 in another. Polyrhythm requires that the four steps are heard *in the same time as* the three. This then generates a composite rhythm ensuing from their interaction within a fixed space.

To illustrate this effect, let us look at the difference between a 4:3 polymeter and a 4:3 polyrhythm in Figure 9.1.

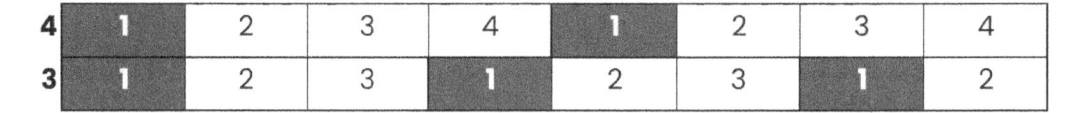

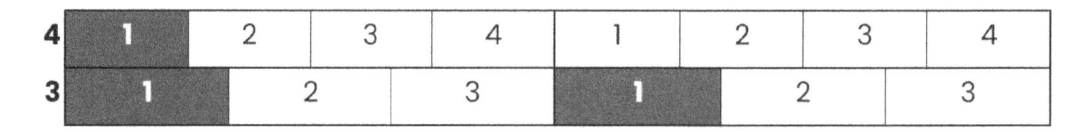

Figure 9.1: In polymeter (top), the rhythmic unit is shared. In polyrhythm (bottom), the bar length is shared.

In short, with polymeter we have:
- Different metric patterns combined;
- Sharing the same rhythmic unit;

- Generating *bars* of different lengths.

The fundamental characteristics of polyrhythm, however, are:
- Different metric patterns combined;
- Sharing the same bar length;
- Generating *rhythmic units* of different lengths.

For the contemporary music producer, polyrhythm provides a brilliant means to expand their roster of rhythmic techniques.

Polyrhythm is prevalent in sub-Saharan Africa, from which the tradition originated. There are two principal forms of polyrhythm used currently:

- Polyrhythm, whereby the effect occurs temporarily.
- Cross-rhythm, whereby the effect occurs throughout the music.

One of the most famous contemporary polyrhythmic records is Babatunde Olatunji's *Drums Of Passion*, which had a profound impact on contemporary American music, particularly jazz.

Elements of polyrhythms

Polyrhythm comprises two elements:

1. The prevailing meter. We know what the prevailing meter is because it's what the dominant elements in the track (e.g. the kickdrum) are working in. If you were using a DAW, it would be the time signature that you set your track to.
2. The variable meter. This is the meter that plays *in addition* to your prevailing meter.

If we refer to our example of a 4/4 meter combined with a 3/4 meter, the way to turn this into a polyrhythm is to stretch or compress the variable meter, lengthening or shortening the notes, so that the two meters have the same length, as seen in Figure 9.2:

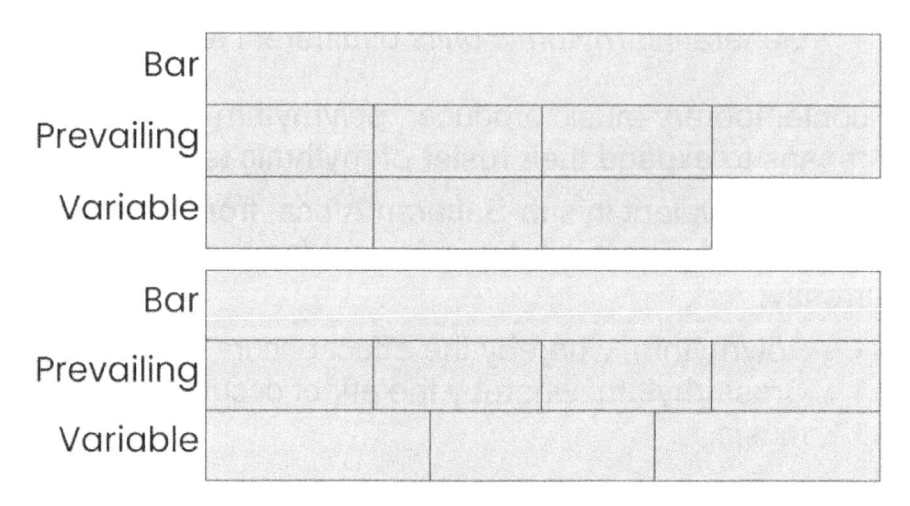

Figure 9.2: To create a polyrhythm, the three-step meter has been stretched to the same length as the four.

As you can see, there are now two meters in play *at the same time* —a 4/4 meter playing with a 3/4 meter. This is a polyrhythm!

Here is another example of a polyrhythm, this time a 4:7. The upper meter is divided into four beats, while the lower meter is divided into seven beats. Notice in Figure 9.3 that while the length of the beats is different, the overall length of the rhythm remains the same:

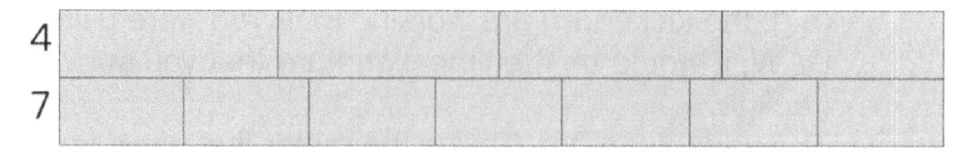

Figure 9.3: A 4:7 polyrhythm.

Remember, of course, that polyrhythms don't simply have to last one bar. They can be as slow or fast as you want—lasting several bars, or fractions of a bar.

A relevant part of the mathematics of polyrhythm is the *resultant cycle*. This is got by multiplying the two cycles together. So, if, for example, you are using a polyrhythm that has a ratio of 4:7, the resultant cycle would be twenty-eight beats long:

Four: 4, 8, 12, 16, 20, 24, **28**, 32, 36, 42

Seven: 7, 14, 21, **28**, 35, 42, 49

The resultant cycle tells you where the polyrhythm repeats—so a 4:7 cycle would repeat after 28 beats of the prevailing meter, or a 3:8 cycle would repeat after 24 beats of the prevailing meter. This is useful to understand the context of your polyrhythm within your wider meter. If, for example, your 3:8 polyrhythm works over sixteenth notes, you know it would repeat every bar and a half in a 4/4 meter (i.e. after 24 sixteenth notes).

Another important feature of a polyrhythm is the composite rhythm. This is the surface rhythm that is produced when all elements of the polyrhythm are playing together. In the example of a 4:7 polyrhythm, the composite rhythm appears as in Figure 9.4:

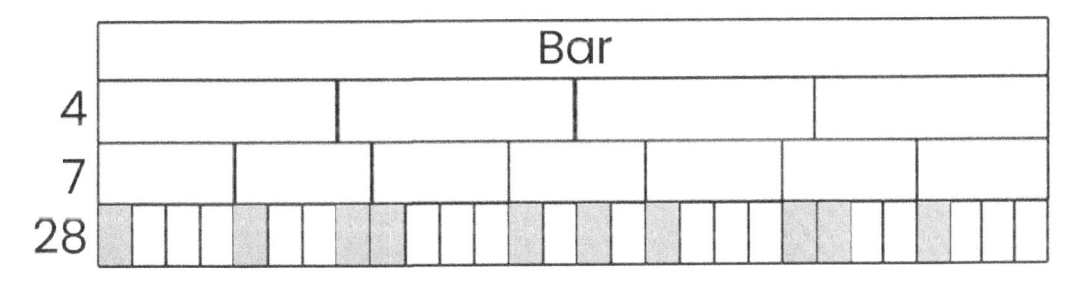

Figure 9.4: Polyrhythms create a 'composite rhythm'—the implied rhythm of both rhythms together.

Once worked out, polyrhythms can then be clapped, giving at least some idea of what the polyrhythm would sound like.

Let's now explore some of the most popular polyrhythms.

3:2 polyrhythms

The simplest polyrhythm is when you combine a meter based on two beats with a meter based on three beats. In effect, this means that one part of the music will be in 2/4 while another part will be in 3/4. This is the most widely known and widely used polyrhythm, known as **hemiola**.

How this polyrhythm is arranged all depends upon the prevailing pulse of the music. If the music is in 2/4, then the other part will appear to be incongruent with it. This is shown in Figure 9.5:

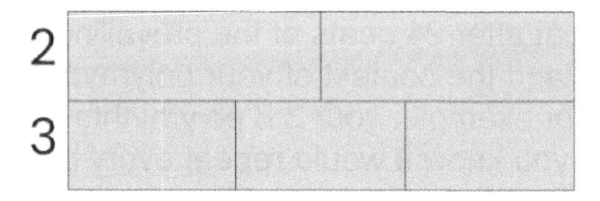

Figure 9.5: If your prevailing meter is 2/4, a 3/4 polymeter will sound incongruent.

However, this doesn't become a problem if you write the lower part using a quarter note triplet grid.

If the prevailing meter of the music is in 3/4 time, the nature of this polyrhythm becomes much easier to understand, see and appreciate. This is because both rhythms will fit into a bar that is six eighth notes long, as shown in Figure 9.6:

Figure 9.6: If the prevailing meter is 3/4, the 2/4 polymeter will sound like compound duple meter (6/8).

Hemiola is a fundamental element in a lot of sub-Saharan African music, and appeared in Western classical music as early as the 15th century.

Hemiola is a great tool to use when you wish to create a sense of rhythmic tension. It sounds like two meters are in conflict, but they resolve elegantly to the listener's ear. A prominent use of hemiola is in *Farmer Refuted* from the Hamilton Musical, whereby Lin-Manuel Miranda and Thayne Jasperson argue. One is in duple meter, the other in triple meter, creating a musical tension between the two parts, signifying their disagreement.

A useful way to gain a better 'feel' for polyrhythms is to learn to play them. Doing so helps you to develop your own sense of polyrhythm. A good way of doing this is to tap your desk in time to the polyrhythm. Assign one rhythm to your right hand and another rhythm to the left hand. Something that helps is the use of a verbal phrase that helps with the precise timing of the beats. So, with hemiola (3:2) you could use a phrase like *'one, two and three'*. This is shown in Figure 9.7:

RH	One		And	
LH	One	Two	Three	

Figure 9.7: A way to articulate hemiola.

Hemiola is unquestionably one of the most fundamental polyrhythms, and a great one to start with when writing music. Consider trying these combinations, one in 2 and the other in 3:

- A bassline and melody
- A hi-hat and ride cymbal
- A sub-bass and drum track

4:3 polyrhythms

Once you've got the hang of hemiola rhythms, you can then become more ambitious. How about using polyrhythms that have a ratio of 4:3? To work out what they would be like, first calculate the length of the resultant cycle, which in this case would be 4×3 which equals 12. Both rhythms could thus be satisfactorily accommodated using a twelve-step cycle. With the 4, that's four sets of 3 steps; while with the 3, that's three sets of four steps. This is seen in Figure 9.8:

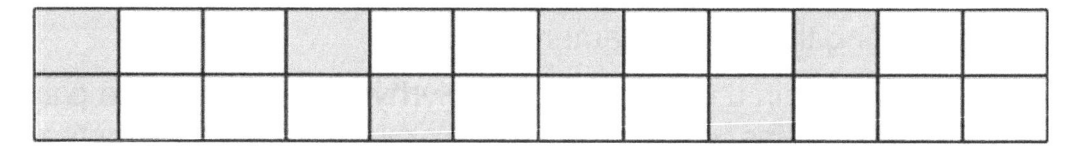

Figure 9.8: The composite rhythm of a 4:3 polyrhythm.

This type of polyrhythm is used extensively in modern jazz, pop and rock music. It was used to impressive effect in some tracks belonging to the appropriately named album Polyrhythm by Peter Magadini. Check out both the *Samba de Rollins* and *Midnight Bolero*. In terms of contemporary electronic music, you can hear a 4:3 polyrhythm at play in *Magnetic Service* by Azu Tiwaline and Cinna Peghamy, or in *Line to earth* by Joe.

When using this type of polyrhythm within your DAW, you're best off creating polyrhythmic patterns using a two-step process:
1. Write your four-beat pattern with the Triplet Grid switched off.
2. Switch Triplet Grid on, and then write your three-beat pattern.

Then it is simply a matter of pressing play, and you will then hear what this polyrhythm sounds like.

You might also want to practise physically playing this polyrhythm. This is more difficult than the 3:2 polyrhythm because the composite rhythm is longer, as well as being more complex and subtle. When trying to play it, remember the order of right hand and left. After the first beat, in which both the right and left hands play, the order is right, left, right, left, right. Also, try using this phrase shown in Figure 9.9: *'I'm feeling good today'*.

RH										
LH										

I'm   fee-ling   good   to-day

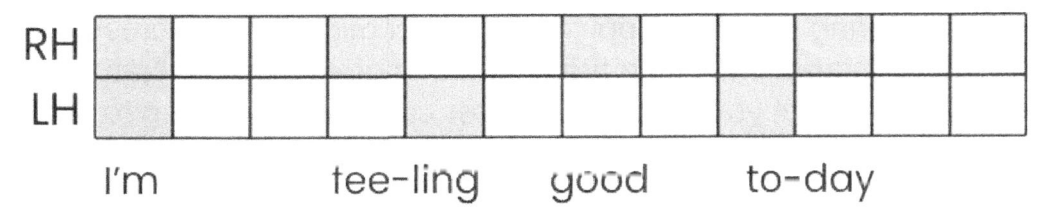

Figure 9.9: A way of articulating a 4:3 polyrhythm.

Once you have mastered the use of 3:2 and then 4:3, you will have a good idea of what is involved when using polyrhythms. Of course, how you use them is down to your own sense of inventiveness and ingenuity. Contexts for their use will no doubt suggest themselves to you once you experiment with them.

More complex polyrhythms

The great thing about polyrhythms is that there is plenty of room for experimentation. This is because, providing the numbers of beats are incongruous with one another, any number of beats can be combined with any other number.

One of my favourites is 5:4 polyrhythms, which are a step up in complexity, when compared to the polyrhythms we've considered so far.

Of course, the larger the numbers of beats, the longer the step cycle that is needed to reconcile both patterns within a single cycle. A great example of this is the 7:4 polyrhythm, as used in the Peter Magadinl's appropriately named track *Seventy-fourth Avenue* from the album Polyrhythm. Listen out for how the drums play within a seven-beat cycle, as other parts play independently within a four-beat cycle.

Use of polyrhythms in DAW software

When exploring the use of polyrhythm, you might come across some difficulties using them within the limitations of your DAW. Naturally, the difficulties that you might encounter can vary according to the polyrhythm. Polyrhythm using numbers such as 3 or 6 present you with few problems, because of the facility of the triplet grid.

In a 4/4 bar, the standard is of course, sixteen steps, each step of which is equivalent to a sixteenth note, as seen in Figure 9.10:

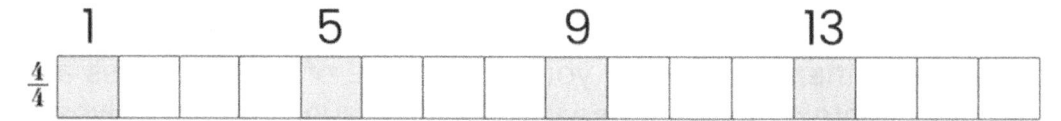

Figure 9.10: Sixteen steps within a bar of 4/4.

For a hemiola polyrhythm, however, enable *Triplet Grid*. When it's enabled, you can easily write in notes in 1/6, 1/12 or 1/24 time; thus creating hemiola, as shown in Figure 9.11:

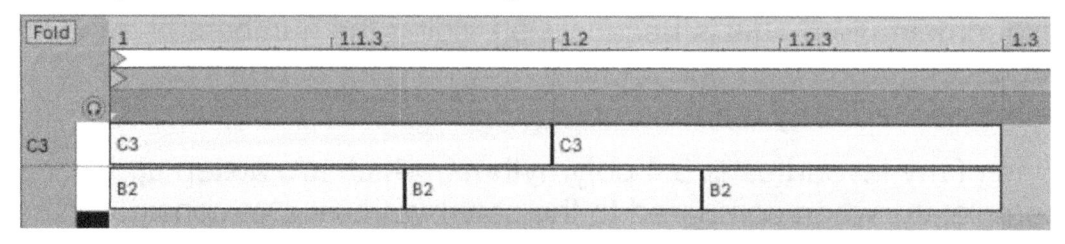

Figure 9.11: The use of Triplet Grid to create hemiola.

However, the more advanced use of polyrhythm, combining many prime numbered cycles, can prove problematic.

Fortunately, most DAW software packages have features that enable clips to be stretched or shrunk.

In this way, a cycle of five beats, for example, can be expanded or contracted to fit into a cycle of eight or four beats, as shown in Figure 9.12:

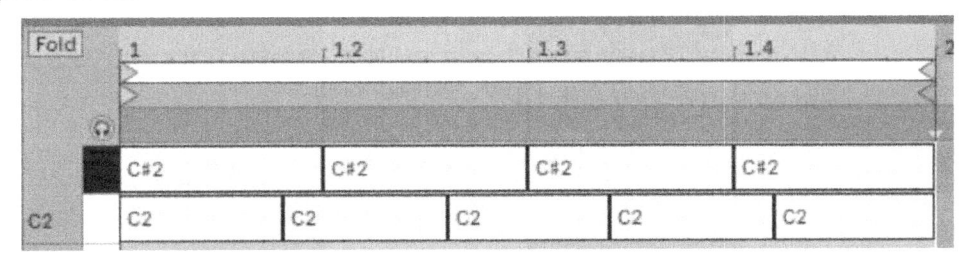

Figure 9.12: Five in the time of four.

To do this, simply follow these step-by-step instructions:

1. Create a MIDI clip of the length of the number of beats you wish to expand or contract in order to fit your prevailing meter. For example, if you're writing a 5:4 polyrhythm, you'll usually want to contract 5 beats into the time of 4—so set your MIDI clip to 5 beats long (or perhaps 5 sub-beats, if you're looking for a shorter polyrhythm). It is a 5-beat polyrhythm we shall create in this example.

2. Add these notes to your MIDI clip.

3. You should now have a pattern that is five beats long, thus lasting one bar and one beat of 4/4 time, as seen in Figure 9.13:

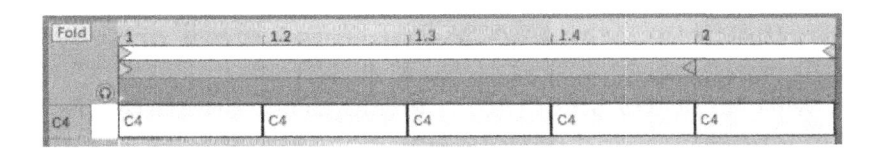

Figure 9.13: Five beats of 4/4 time, five quarter notes in duration.

4. The next step depends on which DAW software you are working in.

   a. If you are using Ableton, select all the notes within your MIDI clip. You should see a little marker appear, as shown in Figure 9.14:

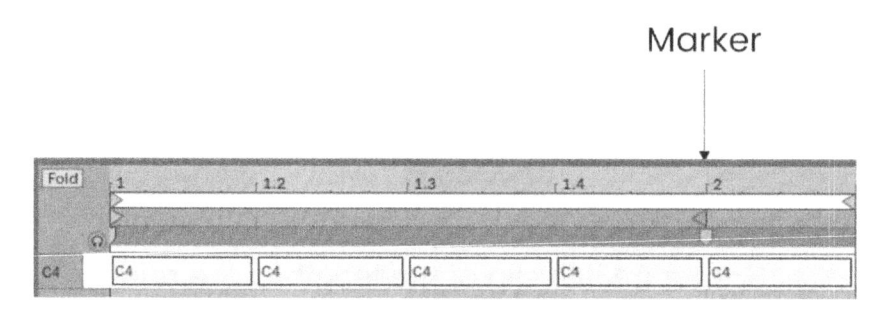

Figure 9.14: A marker appears when all notes are selected.

Hold down Shift, and drag this marker to the end of your five-note clip, as shown in Figure 9.15:

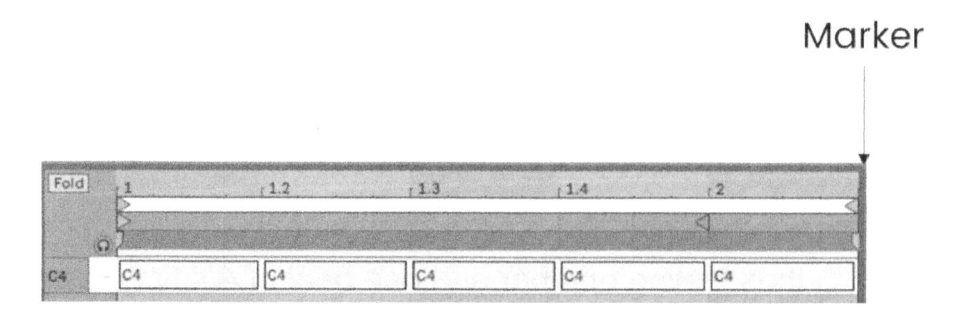

Figure 9.15: While holding shift, drag this marker to the end of the notes you wish to transform into a polyrhythm.

Then, with all notes selected, release Shift, and drag this marker back to where the end of your bar would be if your clip was 4/4, as shown in Figure 9.16:

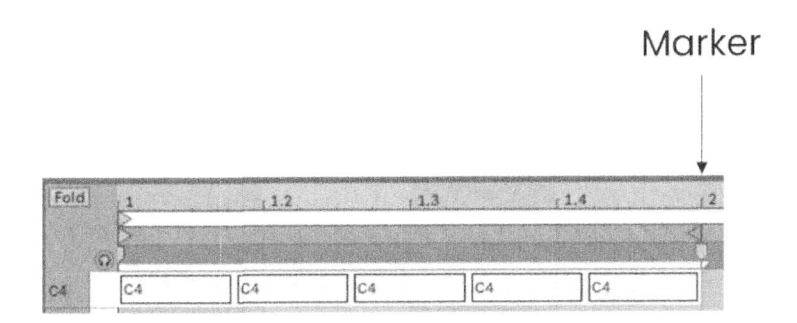

Figure 9.16: Drag this marker back to the end of your 4/4 bar having released Shift.

Now, simply shorten your clip to the length of a 4/4 bar, and there you have it! Five beats in the time of four, as you can see in Figure 9.17:

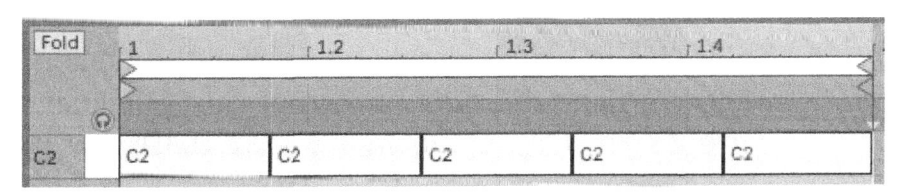

Figure 9.17: Your five beats are now in the time of four.

    b. To do the same in Reason, select the handle at the end of your MIDI clip, and while holding down Ctrl, drag the end of the MIDI clip to the desired size. This will expand or contract your clip, including the events within it. In this way, your clip of five beats length can be contracted into a clip that is four beats long, as seen in Figure 9.18:

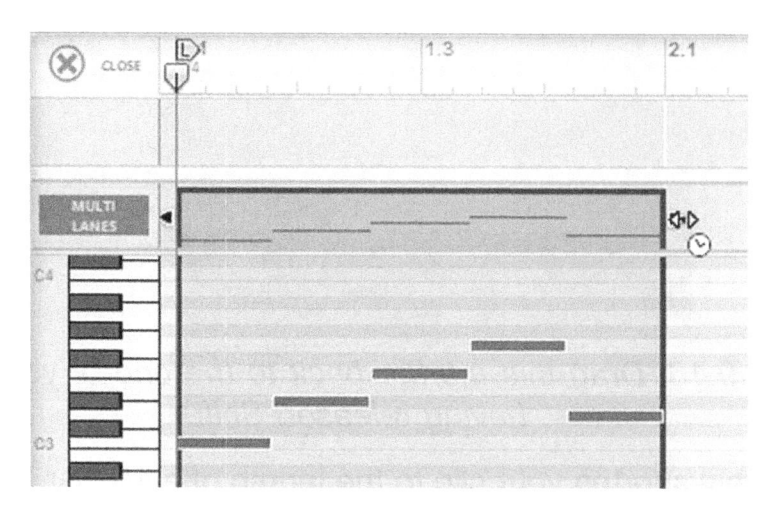

Figure 9.18: The MIDI clip can be expanded or shrunk to create a polyrhythm in Reason.

    c. To do this in Logic, simply hold down the Option key while dragging the right handle of your MIDI clip to the correct size. This is shown in Figure 9.19:

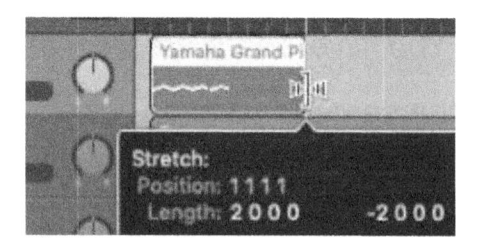

Figure 9.19: Holding down the Option key in Logic will allow you to expand or contract your MIDI clips.

Once you know how to do this, you will then have the complete freedom to use as many polyrhythmic patterns as you want in your work.

Examples of Polyrhythm in Action

In this section, we will look at four simple examples of polyrhythm in action.

You can listen to all these examples at https://meter.producers.guide.

Example One: Shuffled Percussion Track

In this example, I paired a 4/4 garage/electro beat with a Ddjembe and two Brekete drums, as well as a further closed hi-hat loop. This percussion is shown in Figure 9.20:

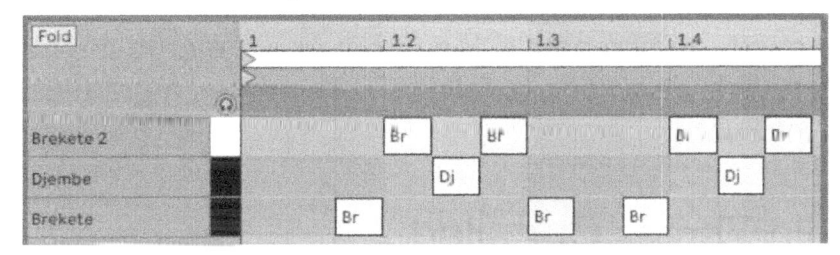

Figure 9.20: A polyrhythmic percussion track.

What made this polyrhythmic is that whereas the beat was written in 4/4 (simple quadruple meter), these drums were written in 12/8 (compound quadruple meter). This imbued the sound with a slightly awkward, shuffling funk.

If you're starting out with polyrhythm, this is the easiest sort of example to follow—it has a big effect on your listener's perception of the rhythm but is easy to achieve—simply switch your grid to Triplet Grid.

Example Two: Triplet Hi-hats vs 4/4 Open Hi-hat

This example is the opposite of the one above. In this, I had a drum track written in compound quadruple meter (12/8), which imbued the drums with a great swing. I therefore added a 909 open hi-hat on the off-beat in 4/4 time (simple quadruple meter), which interrupted the flow of the drums, as shown in Figure 9.21:

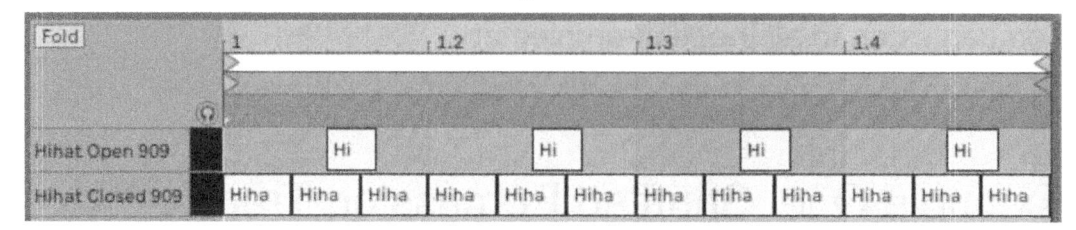

Figure 9.21: The open hi-hat is in simple meter; the closed hi-hat is in compound meter.

This juxtaposition of meters creates an interesting confusion in the listener's mind—they mentally leap from one meter to the other, trying to choose which one to follow. This creates a great deal of rhythmic interest.

Example Three: Curtailed 7:4

In this example, I started with a basic tech-house beat, and added a Roland 303. I spaced the 7 notes of this 303 evenly over the course of one bar, creating a 7:4 polyrhythm, as seen in Figure 9.22:

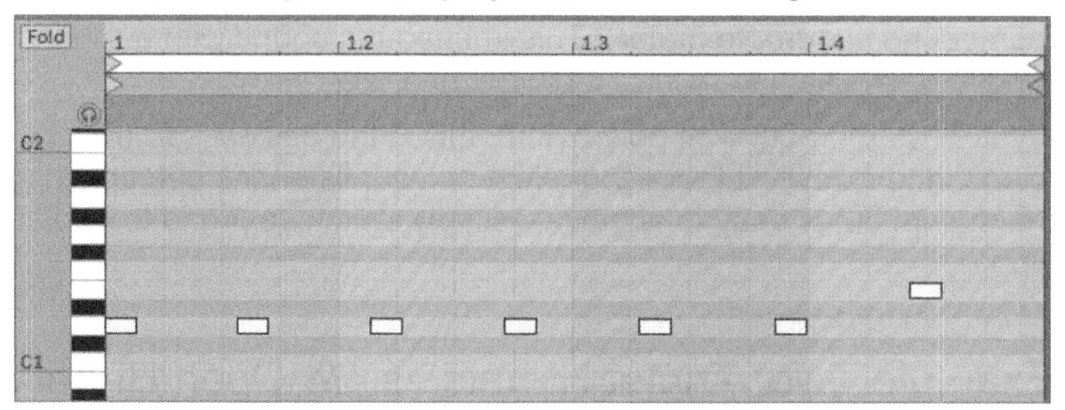

Figure 9.22: A 7:4 polyrhythm.

This created an interesting effect—the first note grounded the listener's expectation of a bar of music that conforms with the prevailing meter, but the remaining notes felt slightly ahead or behind of where they should have been. This push-and-pull effect made the 303 riff feel like it was jutting out from the 4/4 meter, creating a fascinating rhythm.

Example Four: 5 vs 4 vs 3

This example was composed of three elements: the 4/4 drumbeat, a five-step layer and a six-step layer, creating a three-levelled polyrhythm.

The six-step layer was a subtle bleep that, despite being pushed far back in the mix, gave the beat a distinctive swing, framing the other elements with a contrasting 6/8 riff. This is shown in Figure 9.23:

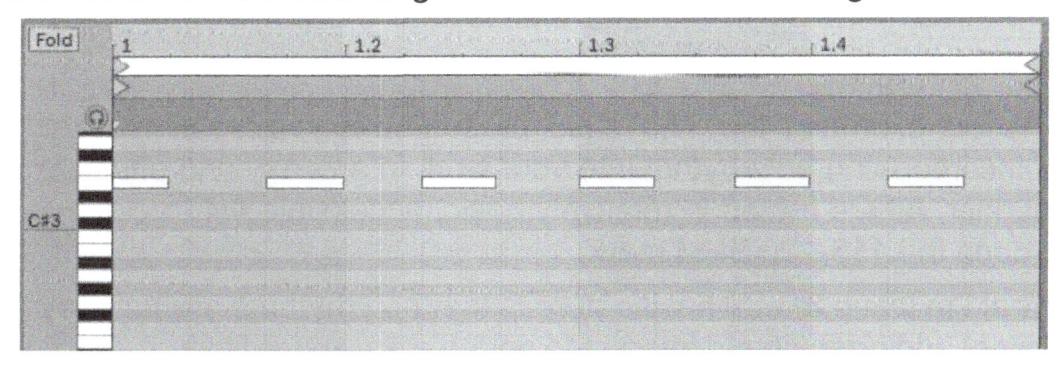

Figure 9.23: The six-step polyrhythmic layer.

The five-step layer was a dub-techno chord, that did a great job of stretching the underlying 4/4. However, I felt that the last beat stretched the underlying meter too far—sounding more like a mistake than an intentional polymeter. I therefore switched the last beat of the 1-bar riff back to 4/4, as shown in Figure 9.24:

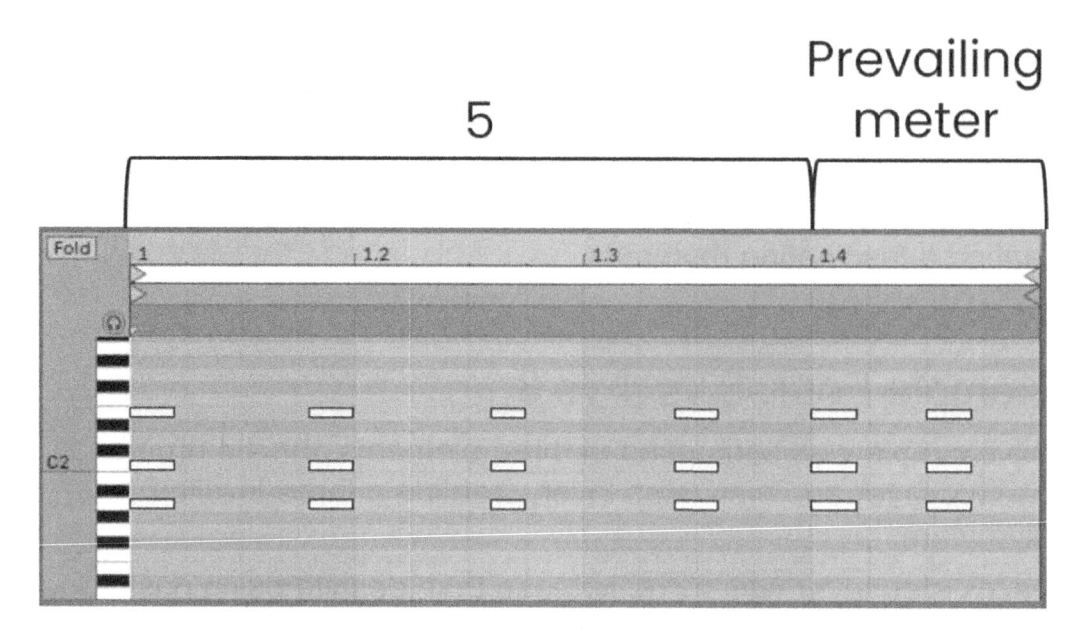

Figure 9.24: The five-step polyrhythm contains one beat of the prevailing meter, in order to ensure that the polyrhythm made enough rhythmic sense to the listener.

The four examples that I have just presented to you are simple ways of incorporating polyrhythm into your work in an easy and effective manner. All are rooted in relatively basic, accessible 4/4 tracks around the 115-130 BPM mark.

What I'm trying to emphasise here is that polyrhythms are an easy way of adding rhythmic interest to your tracks, regardless of which genre you write in. Although many polyrhythmic tracks inhabit a rather narrow niche of musical genres, it doesn't have to be this way. Polyrhythm is a simple rhythmic technique that has been in use for thousands of years of musical history.

Exercises

1. Create a 4/4 drum track.

2. Add a 5/4 polyrhythmic melody, squeezing the five beats into the same time as one bar of 4/4.
3. Add a 12/8 polyrhythmic drum layer (e.g. tambourines or shakers), squeezing these into the same time as one bar of 4/4.

Conclusion

I hope this book has helped build your knowledge of meter, and has provided you with a firm foundation in working with polymeter and polyrhythm.

These are both simple, elegant rhythmic techniques, and I hope you realise that they're easy to put into practice in your work.

You don't have to have an exhaustive knowledge of music theory and music history to use polyrhythm and polymeter; the underlying mathematics are simple.

You equally don't have to base your entire production output on the use of these techniques—merely using them as rhythmic seasoning here and there will be more than enough to give your tracks that extra edge to maintain your listener's interest.

I truly hope the contents of this book have inspired you to create some fantastic music. Thank you for reading it.